Trees for
Southern Landscapes

William D. Adams

Pacesetter Press   A Division of Gulf Publishing Company Houston, Texas

Trees
for
Southern
Landscapes

Trees for
Southern Landscapes

Library of Congress Catalog Card Number 76-15457
ISBN 0-88415-881-0

Designed by Susan Corte
Edited by B.J. Lowe
Illustrated by Terry J. Moore

First Printing, November 1976
Second Printing, May 1980

Acknowledgements

I am especially indebted to Lynn Lowrey and
Lee Marsters for their great interest in woody
plants and for their generosity in sharing this
interest.

Contents

Selecting Trees for Your Landscape, 1

Taking Care of Your Trees, 16

Tree Pests, 30

continued

Southern Landscape Trees, 37

Small to Medium Deciduous Trees, 37

Large Deciduous Trees, 55

Small to Medium Evergreen Trees, 67

Large Evergreen Trees, 71

Palms, 74

Other Landscape Trees, 77

Index, 82

# of special interest...

Climate Data for Southern Cities

	Last Spring Freeze	First Fall Freeze	Frost-Free Days	Record January Low (°F)	Minimum Hours of Chilling	Inches of Rain
Alabama						
Birmingham ..	Mar. 19	Nov. 14	241	1	1,000	53
Huntsville	Apr. 1	Nov. 8	221	−9	1,100	50
Mobile	Feb. 17	Dec. 12	298	14	500	67
Montgomery ..	Feb. 27	Dec. 3	279	5	700	51
Arkansas						
Little Rock	Mar. 16	Nov. 15	244	−4	1,000	49
Florida						
Jacksonville ...	Feb. 6	Dec. 16	313	2	400	53
Orlando	Jan. 31	Dec. 17	319	24	300	51
Tampa.........	Jan. 10	Dec. 26	349	23	200	51
Georgia						
Atlanta	Mar. 20	Nov. 19	244	−3	800	49
Macon	Mar. 14	Nov. 7	240	3	700	44
Savannah	Feb. 21	Dec. 9	291	9	500	48
Kentucky						
Lexington	Apr. 13	Oct. 28	198	−15	1,400	43
Louisville......	Apr. 1	Nov. 7	220	−20	1,400	41
Louisiana						
Baton Rouge ..	Feb. 28	Nov. 30	275	10	500	55
New Orleans ..	Feb. 13	Dec. 9	300	14	400	64
Maryland						
Baltimore	Mar. 26	Nov. 19	238	−7	1,400	43
Mississippi						
Jackson........	Mar. 10	Nov. 13	248	7	700	50
North Carolina						
Charlotte	Mar. 21	Nov. 15	239	4	900	43
Greensboro....	Mar. 24	Nov. 16	237	0	1,100	43
Oklahoma						
Oklahoma City	Mar. 28	Nov. 7	223	0	1,200	32
Tulsa	Mar. 31	Nov. 2	216	−2	1,300	38
South Carolina						
Charleston	Feb. 19	Dec. 10	294	11	600	49
Columbia	Mar. 14	Nov. 21	252	5	700	47
Tennessee						
Knoxville	Mar. 31	Nov. 6	220	−16	1,100	45
Memphis	Mar. 20	Nov. 12	237	−8	1,000	49
Nashville	Mar. 28	Nov. 7	224	−6	1,100	47
Texas						
Austin	Mar. 15	Nov. 20	244	12	700	33
Dallas- Ft. Worth ...	Mar. 18	Nov. 17	244	5	1,000	33
Houston	Feb. 10	Dec. 8	301	19	600	44
San Antonio ...	Feb. 24	Dec. 3	282	0	600	26
Virginia						
Norfolk	Apr. 4	Nov. 9	219	10	1,100	44
Richmond	Apr. 20	Oct. 18	181	−12	1,200	44

Hardiness Zone Map

ZONE 7 0° TO 10°
ZONE 8 10° TO 20°
ZONE 9 20° TO 30°

This map shows in moderate detail the expected minimum winter temperatures in the areas comprising the South. Although this book is applicable to the areas within the bold outline, every gardener should check with his or her local agricultural Extension agent for information on variety selection and availability, and special cultural practices necessary for the particular area.

Horticultural Consultants

Alabama

David Bradford, Extension Horticulturist, Alabama Cooperative Extension Service, Birmingham

Arkansas

Gerald Klingman, Extension Horticulturist, Arkansas Cooperative Extension Service, Fayetteville

Georgia

Troy Keeble, Extension Horticulturist, Georgia Cooperative Extension Service, Atlanta

Louisiana

Severn Doughty, Area Horticulturist, Louisiana Cooperative Extension Service, Metairie

Tom Pope, Extension Horticulturist, Louisiana Cooperative Extension Service, Baton Rouge

Mississippi

James T. Garrett, Leader, Extension Horticulture, Mississippi State University, Mississippi State

North Carolina

Arnold and Connie Krochmal, Agriculture and Science Associates, Asheville

Oklahoma

Raymond Kays, Extension Horticulturist, Oklahoma Cooperative Extension Service, Stillwater

Texas

William D. Adams, Extension Horticulturist, Texas Agricultural Extension Service, Houston

Neal Sperry, Professional Horticulturist, Dallas-Ft. Worth

Terry A. Wilbourn, Extension Horticulturist, Texas Texas Agricultural Extension Service, San Antonio

Selecting Trees for Your Landscape

Southern homeowners are fortunate in that they have a great variety of tree species with which to work. There are a few of the really nice, typically "northern" trees which have no southern counterparts or substitute species. Unfortunately, however, the use of *southern* tree species for home landscaping has not been well documented. Most tree books have been written for the North, with only token mention of southern tree species. As a result, many native trees have been overlooked for

their potential in home landscape use and a great many exotic species are yet to be fully appreciated in southern landscapes.

Along the Gulf Coast and in Florida we certainly don't have the riot of fall foliage color that one might see in the North, but good fall color is possible in almost all areas of the South with trees like Chinese Tallow, Sweetgum, Ash, Crapemyrtle, Blackhaw Viburnum and Drummond Red Maple. These species color well almost every year; other

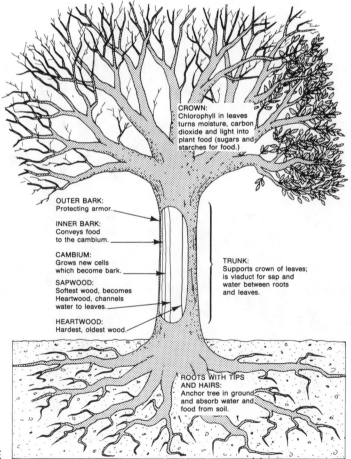

CROWN:
Chlorophyll in leaves turns moisture, carbon dioxide and light into plant food (sugars and starches for food.)

OUTER BARK:
Protecting armor.

INNER BARK:
Conveys food to the cambium.

CAMBIUM:
Grows new cells which become bark.

SAPWOOD:
Softest wood, becomes Heartwood, channels water to leaves.

HEARTWOOD:
Hardest, oldest wood.

TRUNK:
Supports crown of leaves; is viaduct for sap and water between roots and leaves.

ROOTS WITH TIPS AND HAIRS:
Anchor tree in ground and absorb water and food from soil.

THE PARTS OF A TREE

species, like Texas Red Oak, Nuttall Oak, Shumard Oak, Chinese Pistachia and Elm, will color well in most years.

Provenance

Southern gardeners must also consider provenance when selecting trees. *Provenance* refers to the seed source. There is considerable variation in the type of growth and adaptability that a single tree species may have, depending on the origin of the seed. In the South, trees grown from northern seed stock usually grow slowly, come out late in the spring, and are generally unthrifty because their dormancy requirements (sufficient chilling during the winter) are not met. Many tree species, such as red maple, have a wide range of adaptability; however, red maple trees for use in southern landscapes should be grown from parent trees native to a *southern* climate. Some species simply aren't adapted to the South at all, but because they transplant easily and make vigorous growth they're sometimes offered. An excellent example is the Silver Maple (*Acer saccharinum*) which, when grown along the Gulf Coast, at best makes a medium-size tree that eventually becomes a haven for scale insects and diseases.

Variation in seedlings of the same species is illustrated by this planting of Texas Red Oaks.

THE NEED FOR SELECTION AND BREEDING

The South generally is behind when it comes to selection of improved tree varieties. For a number of years our southern lumber companies have been working on pine tree improvement and have made great strides in this area, but the nursery industry is only beginning to be aware of the need for improvement of such stand-by southern trees as the Live Oak, Water Oak, Drummond Red Maple, Arizona Ash, Chinese Tallow Tree, American Elm, Cedar Elm, Bald Cypress, Sweetbay Magnolia, as well as many less common southern trees.

Improved selection and breeding can be achieved in several ways. One way is to produce improved seedling specimens, as we do with annual flowers or vegetables. This technique is much more involved than the asexual propagation of selected plant specimens by budding or grafting, but it has several advantages, including less chance of a build-up of insects and diseases that can wipe out an entire population of identical trees due to a certain amount of variation among the offspring. However, vast numbers of seedling American Chestnuts and American Elms have been lost to single disease problems, Chestnut Blight (*Endothia parasitica*) and Dutch Elm Disease (*Ceratocystis ulmi*), respectively.

Once parent trees have been produced, seedling trees require less labor to produce than grafted trees. Budding and grafting is an expensive procedure which may be increasingly uneconomical in the future. But asexually propagated specimens have advantages, too. For one thing, a number of plant species have both male and female trees. Usually the male tree is preferred for landscape use because the females produce lots of messy fruit or seed pods. Excellent examples are the Ginko, which produces a foul-smelling fruit, and Chinese Pistachia, which simply produces copious quantities of messy fruit. In addition, the latter species seems to have better shape and form in its male trees. With seedling populations of these trees it is generally impossible to tell which are males and which are females until the trees fruit or begin to flower. By this time the plant is well established and essential in the landscape design. Asexually propagated varieties of these species, however, can be entirely male or, if desired, female simply by budding and grafting only from male or female trees.

Almost all landscape trees sold in the South are seedling trees, but they are not from a *selected* seed source, and, in the case of those that produce male and female trees, you won't know what you have until the tree is old enough to begin flowering. Grafted plants sell poorly at nurseries because the public isn't aware of their increased value and is unwilling to pay more money for what *seems* to be a less valuable, smaller plant.

Producing new varieties of trees can certainly be time-consuming and costly. The expense involved in the actual breeding of trees, production of seed, growth of seedlings, and the time required to select outstanding specimens is enormous, not to mention the additional cost of propagation and further testing before they are released to the general public. Then there is the expense of promoting these specimens to make the general public aware of their superior quality. While all this may seem well out of reach of the amateur plant breeder, the sheer lack of competition in the field of ornamental tree genetics makes it a little bit more encouraging. Anyone interested in breeding trees for southern landscapes would do well to consider some of the following genera:

Bauhinia	*Pistachia*
Halesia	*Quercus*
Cercis	*Liquidambar*
Cordia	*Crataegus*
Diospyros	

A faster way to get improved tree specimens for southern landscapes is to select from the large populations of seedling trees that we have already growing. Examples would include all of the native trees as well as Crapemyrtle, Chinese Tallow, Chinese Elm, Callery Pear, Chinese Pistachia, Zelkova, and many other introduced species.

PLANNING

As with most things, some type of a plan—either a formally laid out design or at least a series of statements concerning the type of planting and perhaps the possible planting sites which are suggested for your subdivision—will be a first order of business. When selecting trees for street planting, it is often suggested that, for uniformity, only one plant species be used. However, some variety in planting will add more interest to the subdivision. This does not mean that a columnar tree should be alternated in formal fashion with a spreading tree throughout the subdivision. Rather than attempt some unnatural mixed planting, the best idea is to use either a uniform species planting or to try to arrange the trees as they might be found growing in nature.

How Much is a Tree Worth?

It is difficult to place a dollar value on a tree, but most trees do increase property value. As a guide in determining the value of a shade tree, the International Shade Tree Conference has devised a mathematical means of determining the value of a shade or ornamental tree.

Three basic factors are considered when determining the value of a tree: the size, species, and condition of the tree. Shade tree size is expressed by the cross-sectional trunk area at a point 4½ feet above the ground. To calculate this value, multiply 0.7854 by the square of the diameter. For example, a ten-inch diameter tree has a cross-section area of 78.54 inches. The value given a perfect specimen tree for utilization in this formula is $9.00 per square inch of trunk cross-section (1970).

Not all tree species are of equal value. Trees are divided into five classes based on (a) permanence, (b) pest resistance and low maintenance, (c) natural beauty and landscape quality, (d) cost of replacement, and (e) site adaptability. Each one of these considerations is given a possible point value of 20, and the resulting score is a direct reading of its class. As an example, Live Oak (*Quercus virginiana*) would rate as follows: (a) 20, (b) 18, (c) 18, (d) 15, (e) 18. The total score then is 89, placing the Live Oak in class number I. The material reported and the classifications given to these trees were developed for the South by Dr. Robert S. Dewers, Bexar County Extension Horticulturist, San Antonio, Texas.

CLASS NUMBER I—100%

Carya illinoensis—Pecan
Cornus florida—Flowering Dogwood
Fagus grandifolia—American Beech
Ilex opaca—American Holly
Ilex vornitoria—Yaupon Holly
Liquidambar styraciflua—Sweet Gum
Magnolia grandiflora—Southern Magnolia
Nyssa sylvatica—Tupelo, Blackgum
Quercus alba—White Oak
Quercus macrocarpa—Bur Oak
Quercus muhlenbergii—Chinkapin Oak
Quercus nigra—Water Oak
Quercus shumardii—Shumard Oak
Quercus texana—Spanish Oak
Quercus virginiana—Live Oak
Sophora secundiflora—Mescal Bean Sophora
Taxodium distichum—Bald Cypress
Ulmus crassifolia—Cedar Elm

CLASS NUMBER II—80%

Arbutus texana—Texas Madrone
Carya spp.—Hickories
Diospyros texana—Texas Persimmon
Fraxinus velutina 'glabra'—Modesto Ash
Ginkgo biloba—Ginkgo
Juglans nigra—Black Walnut
Koelreuteria apiculata—Southern Golden Raintree
Koelreuteria paniculata—Panicled Golden Raintree
Lagerstroenia indica—Crapemyrtle
Magnolia virginiana—Sweetbay
Olca manzanilla—Manzanilla Olive
Picca pungens—Colorado Blue Spruce
Pinus edulis—Pinon Pine
Pinus elliottii—Slash Pine
Pinus halepensis—Aleppo Pine
Pinus nigra—Austrian Pine
Pinus ponderosa—Ponderosa Pine
Pinus taeda—Loblolly Pine
Pinus thunbergii—Japanese Black Pine
Pistacia chinensis—Chinese Pistachio
Pithecellobium flexicaule—Texas Ebony
Quercus falcata—Southern Red Oak
Quercus phellos—Willow Oak
Quercus velutina—Black Oak
Ulmus americana—American Elm

CLASS NUMBER III—60%

Acacia farnesiana—Huisache
Acer grandidentatum sinuosum—Bigtooth Maple
Acer rubrum—Red Maple
Betula nigra—River Birch
Cedrus deodara—Deodar Cedar
Chilopsis linearis—Desert Willow
Ehretia anacua—Anaqua
Eriobotrya japonica—Loquat
Fraxinus pennsylvanica lanceolata—Green Ash
Fraxinus velutina (Select Male)—Velvet Ash
Gleditsia triacanthos inermis—Thornless Honeylocust
Gymnocladus dioica—Kentucky Coffeetree
Leucaena pulverulenta—Great Lead-tree
Liriodendron tulipifera—Tulip Poplar
Malus species and varieties—Flowering Crab
Morus alba (fruitless)—Fruitless Mulberry
Persea americana—Avocado
Persea borbonia—Redbay
Pinus echinata—Shortleaf Pine
Pinus pinea—Italian Stone Pine
Platanus occidentalis—American Planetree Sycamore
Prosopis glandulosa—Honey Mesquite
Pyrus calleryana—Calleryana Pear
Quercus stellata—Post Oak
Sapindus drummondii—Western Soapberry
Sophora japonica—Japanese Pagodatree

CLASS NUMBER IV—40%

Acer saccharinum—Silver Maple
Broussonetia papyrifera—Paper Mulberry
Bumellia lanuginosa—Gum Elastic
Celtis occidentalis—Common Hackberry
Cercis spp.—Redbud
Crataegus spp.—Hawthorns
Cupressus arizonica—Arizona Cypress
Firmiana simplex—Chinese Parasol Tree
Fraxinus velutina (seedling)—Arizona Ash
Juniperus spp.—Junipers, Cedar
Maclura pomifera—Bois d'Arc
Prunus blireiana—Ornamental Plum
Prunus mexicana—Mexican Plum
Sapium sebiferum—Chinese Tallow
Ulmus parvifolia sempervirens—Evergreen
   Elm
Zizyphus jujube—Jujube

CLASS NUMBER V—20%

Acer negundo—Boxelder
Ailanthus altissima—Tree of Heaven
Albizia julibrissin—Silktree
Catalpa spp.—Catalpa
Celtis laevigata—Sugarberry
Eleagnus angustifolia—Russian Olive
Melia azedarch—Chinaberry
Morus rubra—Red Mulberry
Parkinsonia aculeata—Palo Verde
Populus spp.—Cottonwood and Poplars
Robinia pseudoacacia—Black Locust
Salix spp.—Willows
Tamarix spp.—Tamarisk
Thuja spp.—Arbor Vitae
Ulmus parvifolia—Chinese Elm
Ulmus pumila—Siberian Elm

Planting distance is important. A general rule of thumb would be 50 to 70 feet apart for large trees, 40 to 50 feet apart for medium-size trees, and 30 to 40 feet apart for small trees. One only has to step into the local woods, though, to see that trees in nature follow no such rule. You may find two beautiful specimens growing only 3 feet apart. Granted, the development of each is influenced by the other, but is that bad? Trees don't have to develop as they would in the middle of an open field to be attractive.

Before selecting a tree species, consider the potential landscape uses you can expect for the tree. Is it a small tree adapted to use as a specimen plant? Can it provide shade? Is it a tree that is especially neat, or will it litter areas like the patio and swimming pool? Can it possibly be used in a container?

Trees for Street Planting

Neighborhoods where relatively insect- and disease-free, long-lived street trees have been planted often retain property values much longer and experience periodic revivals much more so than neighborhoods where faster-growing but shorter-lived trees are planted.

In addition to their aesthetic value, attractive, low-maintenance shade trees along city streets also help to cool the neighborhood by shielding hot sunshine, and they give the community a sense of friendliness and peacefulness that no other physical feature of the landscape can provide.

Many factors must be considered when selecting trees for street planting. Although the initial investment may be of some concern, even more important are the possible maintenance expenses; not only routine maintenance such as pruning and spraying, but the possible maintenance in case of disaster or unsuspected disease or insect problems. Obviously, if we allowed for every possible emergency, perhaps no trees would be planted, yet it's still important to do what can be done well rather than scatter poorly considered, half-hearted attempts over a larger area. In many new developments there is no longer room for giant Live Oak trees. Trees of small or medium stature will be required, and, in most instances, there may be limited area for root and branch development. Utility wires, various other utility easements, water systems, sewage systems, etc., generally take precedence over concern for trees.

Form

Another common omission in tree books, whether written for the North, the South or wherever, is the typical form that a tree species has. Although this form is often variable, some idea of the most common shape of a tree species will be most helpful to anyone working on a landscape design. An actual tree outline for all of the major species of trees discussed in this book is included. Where possible, this outline is of the tree during dormancy. Trees may be open, spreading, columnar, pyramidal, weeping etc.; for those varieties that are known to have various forms, a note to that effect is included in the discussion of the individual tree.

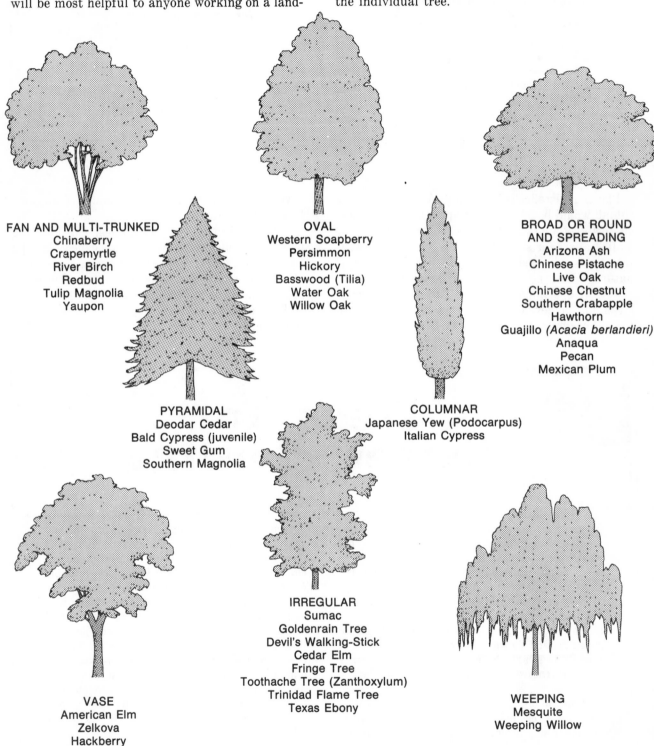

FAN AND MULTI-TRUNKED
Chinaberry
Crapemyrtle
River Birch
Redbud
Tulip Magnolia
Yaupon

OVAL
Western Soapberry
Persimmon
Hickory
Basswood (Tilia)
Water Oak
Willow Oak

BROAD OR ROUND AND SPREADING
Arizona Ash
Chinese Pistache
Live Oak
Chinese Chestnut
Southern Crabapple
Hawthorn
Guajillo *(Acacia berlandieri)*
Anaqua
Pecan
Mexican Plum

PYRAMIDAL
Deodar Cedar
Bald Cypress (juvenile)
Sweet Gum
Southern Magnolia

COLUMNAR
Japanese Yew (Podocarpus)
Italian Cypress

VASE
American Elm
Zelkova
Hackberry
Texas Sophora

IRREGULAR
Sumac
Goldenrain Tree
Devil's Walking-Stick
Cedar Elm
Fringe Tree
Toothache Tree (Zanthoxylum)
Trinidad Flame Tree
Texas Ebony

WEEPING
Mesquite
Weeping Willow

SOME BASIC TREE FORMS

Leaves

In addition to utility and form, there are several other important questions you should ask yourself when selecting a particular tree species for your landscape. About leaves, for instance; consider their overall texture—does the plant look coarse like a catalpa tree, or is it fine-textured like a mimosa? Does the foliage have color, like some of the purple-leaved plums and crabapples? Are the leaves messy? Large-leaved trees tend to be messier. This often goes along with texture.

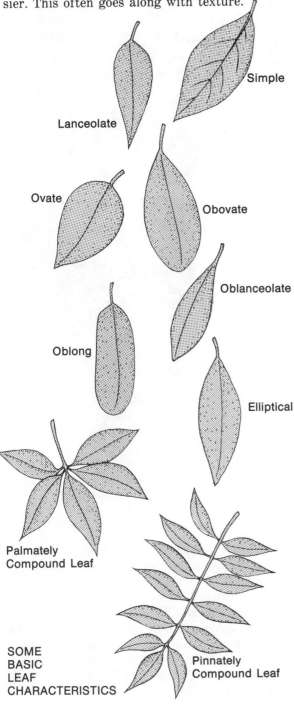

Lanceolate

Simple

Ovate

Obovate

Oblanceolate

Oblong

Elliptical

Palmately Compound Leaf

Pinnately Compound Leaf

SOME BASIC LEAF CHARACTERISTICS

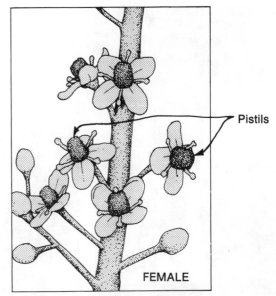

Pistils

FEMALE

Sex expression in tree flowers: male flowers have well-developed stamens with only rudimentary pistils; females have well-developed pistils with rudimentary stamens.

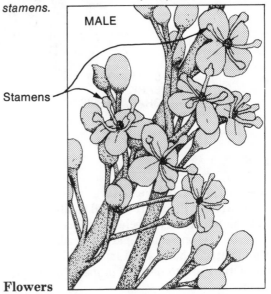

MALE

Stamens

Flowers

Flowers are particularly important if the tree is being planted as a specimen tree. When does it flower? Does it have male and female flowers? What color are they? Can you expect messy seed or perhaps very attractive seed pods, such as those of the Golden Rain Tree?

Bark

The tree bark is also important. Many trees have an attractive bark color. The Japanese Crapemyrtle, with its cinnamon-red bark, is a good example. Bark that peels (exfoliates) is also attractive in many species, especially River Birch and the true Chinese Elm (*Ulmus parvifolia*).

Hybrid Crapemyrtle

Juniper

STRIKING
BARK
CHARACTERISTICS

River Birch

True Chinese Elm

Light

A tree's required light exposure is also important. Some trees will endure partial shade, in fact, many of the understory species, such as Dogwood and Silverbell, even require partial shade. Others may stand partial shade while small but must have full sun if they are to develop properly once they get larger.

Soil

The tree's soil requirements are important too. Generally, a tree has to adapt to the soil in your landscape; but there are special situations, as with small- to medium-sized trees, where you may want to construct a special bed. Dogwood trees, for example, simply won't grow in tight wet soils in a full sun exposure, but by preparing a planting bed much like you would for camellias you'll have excellent results. Some trees are rather tolerant of salt, and so they are better adapted for seashore areas. Trees that are adapted to dry western climates often can be used in easterly high rainfall areas simply by planting them high in raised beds.

Longevity

Don't forget to consider the life expectancy of the tree. Though almost all homeowners initially ask for a tree that's fast-growing, it's important to note that most fast-growing trees don't live very long (Arizona Ash and Fruitless Mulberry, for example). A tree that only lives 20 to 30 years becomes a liability just about the time it reaches maturity. On the other hand, many of the oaks and longer-lived trees continue to increase in value throughout their life.

Poisonous Leaves and Berries

It would be a dull world if we eliminated all the poisonous plants, but this is something to consider when selecting trees. Perhaps just as annoying as the threat of a possible poisoning are trees like the Chinaberry tree and the Western Soapberry, which produce messy berries that children are fond of throwing. Both types are otherwise desirable for landscape use.

Roots

The type of root system that a tree develops is also important. Many of the Chinese Tallow, Ash, Mulberry and other vigorous trees have such shallow, competitive roots that they not only kill out the grass but also tend to enlarge and protrude above the surface of the soil. The problem is severe in tight soils because the roots tend to develop close to the surface where there is a higher concentration of oxygen.

Hardiness

Hardiness is difficult to define and even more difficult to specify for a particular species because so many factors determine the hardiness of a tree in relation to temperature. Trees that ordinarily stand 0°F may die at 12°F if this temperature comes suddenly and at the end of an active growing period. This is a common problem with such tree species as Eucalyptus in the southeast. They grow so well here that they have trouble slowing down and getting ready for cold weather.

Tree hardiness is determined by a number of other factors, too. Hardiness refers not only to a plant's resistance to cold but also to its ability to withstand the stresses of pollution, drought, insect and disease damage, poor drainage, salt in the wind (and in the soil for seaside plantings) and any other factors that can influence the tree's health. If, for example, it is known that a tree is "hardy to Zone 7" on the USDA Plant Hardiness Map, this tree will survive in Zone 7 and further south until some other factor, such as inadequate winter chilling, limits its growth.

Trees develop resistance to cold injury by becoming dormant during the winter. This dormancy is brought about primarily by two factors (1) reduced temperatures and (2) shorter daylength (a photoperiod response. A reduction in the amount of water may also help to bring on dormancy). "Hardy" trees that in an ordinary winter require gradually cooler temperatures may die when a warm fall is followed by a sudden hard freeze. It is important to reduce watering in late fall and, of course, not to apply fertilizer around tender trees any later than mid-summer. Some trees, such as citrus, are worth going to a little extra effort for on those one or two nights when a hard freeze may spoil all your plans for next year's harvest. Some people even go to the trouble of building a frame around the tree and covering this frame with plastic when a hard freeze is anticipated. Inclusion of a small bathroom heater in this enclosure will protect citrus on all but the coldest nights. If you simply want to keep the tree from dying back beyond the graft union, wrapping the trunk with foam rubber or thick layers of newspaper will usually provide sufficient insulation to prevent damage to the trunk. At least when the tree sprouts back out again it will be possible to promote growth from the portion above the graft.

Other factors influencing hardiness may be imposed by the gardener: fertilizer application late in the season which may prolong growth, outside lighting that may prevent the tree from triggering a dormancy phase, excessive watering late in the season, or damage to the tree, such as that experienced in home construction, may combine to make an otherwise hardy tree die when ordinarily it shouldn't.

In relating hardiness to a map, again, there are always microclimates—perhaps at a higher elevation, a location in a valley, or a location influenced by a body of water—that can support plants which otherwise would be too tender to survive (see USDA Plant Hardiness Map, page ix).

CHARACTERISTICS OF SOME POPULAR LANDSCAPE TREES

The following tree lists are intended as a handy "quick reference" when selecting trees for your landscape. After deciding on several potential choices, check the individual descriptions of trees (pages 37-81) for more detailed information.

SMALL FLOWERING TREES

Name	Flower Color
Redbud (*Cercis canadensis*)	pink or white
Trinidad Flame Tree (*Calliandra guildingi*) (tweedii)	red
Red Buckeye (*Aesculus pavia*)	red
Texas Sophora (*Sophora affinis*)	light lavender
Guajillo (*Acacia berlandieri*)	yellow
Anacacho Bauhinia (*Bauhinia congesta*)	white
White Flowered Bauhinia (*Bauhinia forficata*)	white
Fringetree (*Chionanthus virginicus*)	white
Parsley Hawthorn (*Crataegus marshalli*)	white
May Haw (*Crataegus opaca*)	white

Tulip Magnolia (*Magnolia soulangeana*)	pink
Wild Olive (*Cordia Boissieri*)	white
Geiger-Tree (*Cordia sebestena*)	red
Trifoliate Orange (*Poncirus trifoliata*)	white
Serviceberry (*Amelanchier arborea*)	white
Mexican Plum (*Prunus mexicana*)	white
Prairie Crabapple (*Malus ioensis*)	pink
Virginia Stewartia (*Stewartia malacodendron*)	white
Two-Wing Silverbell (*Halesia diptera*)	white
Southern Blackhaw Viburnum (*Viburnum rufidulum*)	white
Citrus	
Kumquat (*Fortunella*)	white
Satsuma (*Citrus*)	white
Tangerine (*Citrus*)	white
Orange (*Citrus*)	white
Lemon (*Citrus*)	white
Grapefruit (*Citrus*)	white
Tree Huckleberry (*Vaccinium arboreum*) (Farkleberry)	white
Florida Anisetree (*Illicium floridanum*)	red
Lilac Chastetree (*Vitex agnuscastus*)	lavendar

MEDIUM-SIZE FLOWERING TREES

Name	Flower Color
Huisache (*Acacia farnesiana*)	yellow
Southern Golden Raintree (*Koelreuteria bipinnata*) (*apiculata*)	yellow
Panicled Golden Raintree (*Koelreuteria paniculata*)	yellow
Crapemyrtle (*Lagerstroemia indica*)	white, red, pink, lavendar
Japanese Crapemyrtle (*Lagerstroemia fauriei*)	white
Hybrid Crapemyrtle [*Lagerstroemia (fauriei X indica)*]	white, pink, lavendar
Jerusalem Thorn (*Parkinsonia aculeata*)	yellow
Tung-Oil Tree (*Aleurites fordii*)	reddish-white
Common Pear (*Pyrus communis*)	white
Evergreen Pear (*Pyrus kawakami*)	white
Callery Pear (*Pyrus calleryana*)	white
Southern Crabapple (*Malus angustifolia*)	pink
American Yellow Wood (*Cladrastis lutea*)	white

LARGE FLOWERING TREES

Name	Flower Color
Drummond Red Maple (*Acer rubrum drommondii*)	red
Tulip Tree (*Liriodendron tulipfera*)	orange and green
Sweet Bay Magnolia (*Magnolia virginiana*)	white
Southern Magnolia (*Magnolia grandiflora*)	white

TREES WITH FRAGRANT FLOWERS

Loquat (*Eriobotrya japonica*)
Plums (especially Mexican Plum) (*Prunus mexicana*)
Huisache (*Acacia farnesiana*)
Crapemyrtle (some) (*Lagerstroemia indica*)
Guajillo (*Acacia berlandieri*)
Trifoliate Orange (*Poncirus trifoliata*)
Texas Persimmon (*Diospyros texana*)
Sweet Bay Magnolia (*Magnolia virginiana*)
Banana Shrub (*Michelia figo*)
Citrus
   Kumquat (*Fortunella margarita*)
   Satsuma (*Citrus*)
   Tangerine (*Citrus*)

Grapefruit (*Citrus*)
Meyer Lemon (*Citrus*)
Orange (*Citrus*)
Southern Magnolia (*Magnolia grandiflora*)
Fringetree (*Chionanthus virginicus*)
Tuliptree (*Liriodendron tulipifera*)

TREES WITH AROMATIC FOLIAGE

Deodar Cedar (*Cedrus deodara*)
Camphor Tree (*Cinnamomum camphora*)
Silver Dollar Eucalyptus (*Eucalyptus cinera*)
Southern Waxmyrtle (*Myrica cerifera*)

SMALL UNDERSTORY TREES

(These Trees Tolerate Partial Shade and Need a Loose, Acid Soil)

Dogwood (*Cornus florida*)
Fringetree (*Chionanthus virginicus*)
Mayhaw (*Crataegus opaca*)
American Holly (*Ilex opaca*)
Possumhaw Holly (*Ilex decidua*)
Dahoon Holly (*Ilex cassine*)
Star Magnolia (*Magnolia stellata*)
Tulip Tree (Deciduous Magnolia) (*Magnolia soulangeana*)
Carolina Buckthorn (*Rhamnus caroliniana*)
Anisetree (*Illicium*)
Wax Myrtle (*Myrica cerifera*)
Red Buckeye (*Aesculus pavia*)
Shadbow Serviceberry (*Amelanchier arborea*)
American Hornbeam (*Carpinus caroliniana*)
American Hop-Hornbeam (*Ostrya virginiana*)
Silverbell (*Halesia diptera*)
Blackhaw Viburnum (*Viburnum rufidulam*)

TREES FOR SOUTHERN SEASHORES

Arizona Ash (*Frafinus velutina*)
Southern Magnolia (*Magnolia grandiflora*)
Olive (*Olea europala*)
Aleppo Pine (*Pinus halapensis*)
Maritime Pine (*Pinus pinaster*)
Wild Blackcherry (*Prunus serotina*)
Live Oak (*Quercus virginiana*)
Texas Palmetto (*Sabal texana*)
Chinese Elm (*Ulmus parvifolia*)
Washingtonia Palm (*Washingtonia filifera*)

TREES FOR MOIST SOILS

May Haw (*Crataegus opaca*)
Trifoliate Orange (*Poncirus trifoliata*)
Southern Waxmyrtle (*Myrica cerifera*)
River Birch (*Bretula migra*)
Drummond Red Maple (*Acer rubrum drummondi*)
Black Gum (Tupelo) (*Nyssa sylvatica*)
Water Oak (*Quercus nigra*)
Willow Oak (*Quercus phellos*)
Baldcypress (*Taxodium distichum*)
Montezuma Boldcypress (*Taxodium mucronatum*)
Sweet Bay Magnolia (*Magnolia virginiana*)
Overcup Oak (*Quercus lyrata*)
Swamp Chestnut Oak (*Quercus prinus*)
Laurel Oak (*Quercus laurifolia*)

HOW TO TRANSPLANT TREES

Planting Bare-Root Trees

When planting bare-root trees, dig a hole large enough to allow the root system to spread naturally. It is not necessary to dig the hole much larger. Check the root-packing material to make sure it is moist, and don't allow the roots to dry out. If you plan to plant within the next few hours, soak the roots in a pail of water during this time. If it will be several days before you plant, dig a shallow trench and "heel in" the plants.

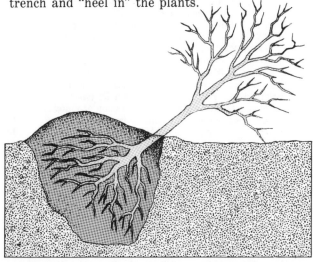

If it will be several days before you can plant your bare-root tree, heal-in the transplant with moist soil to prevent drying of the roots.

Before planting, cut back any broken or damaged roots. Mound good topsoil in the bottom of the hole to form a cone on which to spread the root system. Backfill the hole three-fourths full, working the soil firmly around the root system with your fingers to eliminate air pockets. Fill the hole with water and let settle. This should eliminate any remaining air pockets. Finally, add the remaining topsoil. Unless the topsoil is very deep, it may be advantageous to add organic matter, about one-third by volume, to the soil used as backfill. Watering can be facilitated by creating a watering basin with the extra soil mix. In areas of high rainfall and poor drainage, the watering basin may cause more problems that it is worth.

Planting B & B or Canned Nursery Stock

Balled and burlapped trees, as well as those grown in containers, have an advantage over bare-root trees in that their root systems are relatively undisturbed. So avoid breaking or damaging the root ball to get the best performance from B & B

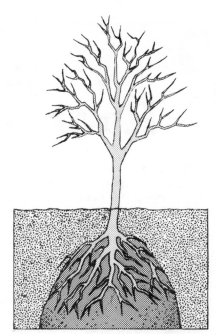

Before planting, mound good topsoil in the bottom of the planting hole to form a cone on which to spread the root system.

trees. Most nursery stock of this type can be planted any time of the year.

Occasionally you may buy a tree that has been growing in a container too long and has become root-bound. This condition is characterized by a mass of roots spiraled around the bottom and sides of the container and usually growing out of the drainage holes. In addition, the plant usually appears stunted. Begin by thoroughly soaking the root ball. Let it stand several hours in a pan of water or comletely immerse it for about 15 minutes. Unless you pry and loosen this root mass or cut some roots, the plant will probably never outgrow this condition. If you have to damage or remove part of the root system, you will need to compensate by pruning off about one-third of the top growth. *(Text continued on next page)*

When you see roots beginning to grow out of the drainage holes of the pot and/or if your seedling or potted tree appears stunted, the plant is root-bound—it's time to transplant.

About Rooting Hormones

The following comments from Dr. Bruno C. Moser, Head, Department of Horticulture, Purdue University, summarize the results of some of the current work which he is now heading involving auxin (rooting hormone) effects on root regeneration when transplanting difficult woody species.

As noted by Dr. Moser, the concentration required to stimulate root regeneration on the test plants was rather high. A locally available root stimulator and starter solution contains only .004% indole-3-butyric acid, which, even in the concentrated solution form, is well below the recommended rate. The directions for use of this product suggest a further dilution of 1 to 76 which would make the concentration of root hormone rather insignificant according to Dr. Moser's work. This root stimulator also contains a 5-20-10 fertilizer which may be of some aid in helping the plant to get started, but the value of this fertilizer in root re-generation or in easing transplanting shock is also questionable.

"Most of the work that we have been doing is on the effects of auxins in stimulating root regeneration of transplanted scarlet oak. After investigating several different auxins it is apparent that both IBA and NAA at 3000 parts per million will result in a stimulation of root initiation when roots of transplanted trees are dipped into these solutions. NAA would be more appropriate than IBA as the cost of the chemical is considerably less. Roots dipped in these auxins resulted in significantly increased total root number and length when compared with untreated plants under field conditions. Another treatment, employing toothpicks impregnated with 1000 parts per million IBA solution and inserted into tap roots of one year old scarlet oak seedlings, resulted in even greater increases in total root number and length than dipping the roots in auxin solutions. The major effect of auxin treatment to scarlet oak root systems is to stimulate the regeneration of many more roots than would normally be formed. The treatment does not shorten the time to first root regeneration nor does it effect rate of root elongation.

There is no question that plants treated with auxins to stimulate root regeneration have a more extensive root system and should be able to survive stress conditions more readily than plants that have not received the auxin treatment."

Note: a 1000 ppm solution can be obtained by dissolving 1 gram of a 100% active ingredient material in one liter of water. Less concentrated materials would, of course, require more than 1 gram. For instance, an 80% active ingredient material would require 1.25 grams (.8 x 1.25 = 1).

(Text continued)

Dig the hole no deeper than is necessary to set the plant at its original soil level or slightly higher (1 to 2 inches) and 12 to 18 inches wider than the root ball. When planting in a sandy soil, save the topsoil and mix it 1:1 with organic matter such as peat moss, pine bark or compost. Utilize this mixture to backfill the hole.

If the soil is a tight clay, backfill with the original clay topsoil. Organic matter may be mixed in, but in areas with high rainfall and poor drainage, reserve this mixture for the final ⅓ of the backfill. Firm the soil but do not pack it, especially if it's tight clay.

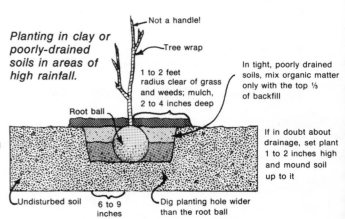

Planting in sandy, well-drained soils or in areas of low rainfall.

Not a handle!
Tree wrap
1 to 2 feet radius clear of grass and weeds
Mulch 2 to 4 inches deep
Mound of soil to form a watering basin
Root ball
Dig hole no deeper than necessary to set the plant at its original soil level.
Mix backfill 1:1 with organic matter
6 to 9 inches
Dig planting hole wider than the root ball

Planting in clay or poorly-drained soils in areas of high rainfall.

Not a handle!
Tree wrap
1 to 2 feet radius clear of grass and weeds; mulch, 2 to 4 inches deep
Root ball
In tight, poorly drained soils, mix organic matter only with the top ⅓ of backfill
If in doubt about drainage, set plant 1 to 2 inches high and mound soil up to it
Undisturbed soil
6 to 9 inches
Dig planting hole wider than the root ball

With the hole ¾ full, water thoroughly to settle the soil around the roots. A root starter may be used but it is not absolutely necessary.

In an area with as many variations in soil conditions, climate and topography as the South, it is difficult to give general instructions without mentioning exceptions. Some of these are described below.

Time of Year:
Summer—may need watering basin, even along the Gulf Coast.
Winter—knock down any watering basin if season is rainy and drainage is poor.

Type of Plant:
Some plants, such as willow, baldcypress and other wetland species, will tolerate poor drainage. Others, such as the pecan, require special planting techniques.

Topography:
If plants are on a definite slope, drainage is not a problem even with tight soil and high rainfall.

Climate:
Areas of low rainfall definitely need a watering basing plus the addition of more organic matter to help hold moisture. This is particularly true where this condition is combined with poor soil.

Plants larger than 4 feet require staking or guy wiring, particularly if grown in an area exposed to frequent winds. Trees up to 20 feet may be supported with one or two strong stakes driven several feet into the ground approximately one foot away from the trunk. The stake should extend at least to the first branches after being driven into the ground. Attach the tree to the stakes with a wire enclosed in a length of old garden hose. Heavily branched and dense trees within this size range may require guying.

Guy wires must be used to support larger trees. Use at least three wires spaced at even intervals around the tree. Attach the wires with wire loops. Be sure to protect the bark from abrasion by enclosing the wire where it circles the tree in a length of old garden hose. Keep wires taut by occasionally readjusting the tension.

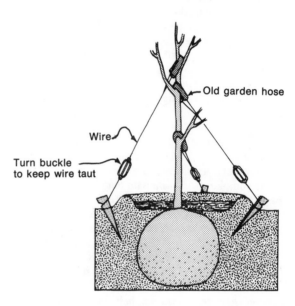

Guy wire supports should be used to support larger transplants.

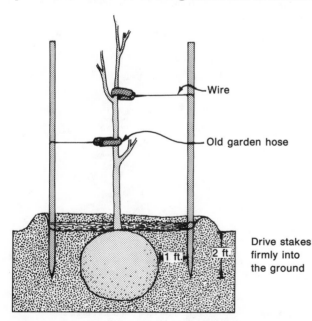

Supporting transplants with stakes. This method is suitable for light- to medium-branched trees up to 20 feet.

Encourage a deep root system by watering thoroughly. Frequent watering is necessary for the first few weeks, particularly in the summer, but once the tree roots become establishd allow the soil to dry slightly and then soak at least to the depth of the root ball.

If the tree has sparse foliage and is subjected to full sun, wrap the trunk to prevent sun scalding. Special tree wrap paper is available from most garden centers; strips of burlap also can be used to shade the trunk. Aluminum foil is great for this purpose; it is an excellent heat reflector, it is easy to use, and it protects the bark against rodent damage. A 3 to 4-inch mulch extending in a radius 1 to 2 feet around the base of the tree helps conserve moisture and reduces competition from weeds.

Transplanting Trees from the Wild

Trees such as dogwoods, oaks and many pines usually die when transplanted from the woods unless you use care in handling them. To insure a better chance of success, it's advisable to root prune the plants prior to digging.

Root pruning involves cutting all the roots with a sharp spade at the same distance from the trunk as when you're digging a root ball. Dig out from the trunk one foot for each inch diameter of the trunk before you start cutting the roots. Next, make sure the roots beneath the plant are also cut. Then lift the plant slightly to make sure that all the roots are free, drop the plant back into position, firm the soil around it, and see that it is watered during dry periods. Though most plants can be successfully transplanted this way, the plants that have very dominant tap roots such as hickory and sassafras, may not survive.

If you plan to dig the wild plant in the dormant season (the best time), you need to do the root pruning the previous spring. Even if extensive root pruning is not possible (for example, cutting under all the roots) if you at least cut some of the lateral roots in the outline of the proposed planting ball, you'll make the tree easier to transplant.

When the time comes to actually move the tree out of the wild, dig the soil ball with a sharp shovel using care to dig in a circular motion and not with leverage against the root ball. Once you've completely outlined the sides of the root ball, you can begin to undercut it and prepare to move it out of its original position and into the landscape. A large piece of burlap is helpful in insuring that the move from the wild to your home will not break up and damage the soil ball. Simply roll up the burlap above half way, place the roll at the bottom of the hole, tip the soil ball to one side and slip the roll under as much as possible, then tip it to the other side and pull the roll through so that you have gone completely under the soil ball, and secure this as tightly as possible over the top of the soil ball and handle the plant by the soil ball rather by the trunk or limbs. Once the plant has been successfully transplanted, prune it back about one-third to one-half. This pruning may be done prior to moving if the removal of some of the branches will make the tree easier to handle. If the root ball should break during removal don't give up. It's amazing how easily some plants are transplanted, even without prior root pruning. This especially true of smaller plants.

The key to success where you've had root damage or where you're bare-rooting trees (this is generally only advisable with deciduous trees) is pruning back some of the top to compensate for the loss of root system. Also, it's important not to allow the root system to dry out during the transplanting phase.

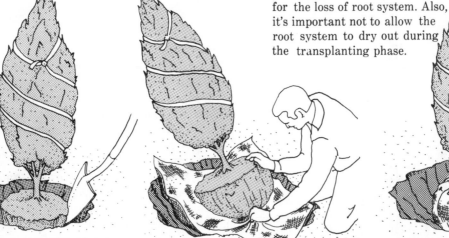

The radius of the soil ball should be one foot for each inch of trunk diameter. Dig with the back of the spade toward the plant to avoid prying up uncut roots. After the rootball is cut, trim and shape the ball, and undercut the roots.

Tip the ball and tuck a roll of burlap under it. Tip the ball in the opposite direction; unroll and pull the burlap under the ball.

Pin the burlap together with nails. If the soil is especially dry and crumbling, further secure the burlap with a nylon cord or small rope. Do not lift the plant by its trunk or branches. Lift small plants by the rootball and larger ones by prying up with 2 spades.

Instant Trees

In most larger cities it is possible to purchase large trees which are transplanted from the wild with the use of special digging equipment. Since the development of this type of equipment it has been possible to have almost instant shade. The larger machines can remove as much as a 72-inch diameter root ball, and a tree up to 10-inches in diameter can be successfully transplanted using this technique. Besides the obvious advantage of having a very large tree which provides almost immediate mature tree effect, there's the possibility of getting outstanding native plant specimens like Cedar Elm, Live Oak and various other trees that the tree mover may have special permission to dig from nearby fields, and even though trees may be rather expensive, anywhere from $400 to $1500 or more, the extra money spent is an excellent investment if the tree planted is a long-lived species that will continually add to the value of the landscape.

Some special care is needed, but much of this will have already been done by the tree transplanting company. Trees such as Live Oaks, for instance, may have many or all of their leaves stripped during transplanting, especially if the transplanting is done later in the growing season. Most trees will be pruned back one-third to as much as one-half to compensate for the loss in root system. About all you'll have to do is insure that the rootball doesn't dry out during the establishment of one to two years. Because of the large size of this root ball, it will probably be necessary to use an instrument such as an iron rod to probe the soil in the root ball and in the area immediately adjacent to the root ball to determine whether or not it is moist. If the rod is easily pushed into the soil, the soil should be damp enough. If, on the other hand, when you push the rod into the soil 6 to 12 inches and it suddenly resists further movement, chances are the soil is dry below this area. Allowing the water to trickle at a very slow rate at the base of the tree where it will gradually soak deep into the root zone area is advisable when watering is necessary. But, at the same time, overwatering or a constant waterlogging of the soil should also be avoided. If you make a small dike of soil to retain water around the tree initially and during dry periods, you'll probably be better off by eliminating this water-retaining barrier when rains are more frequent.

Fully-grown trees are easily transplanted with the aid of a commercial transplanter. This service is somewhat expensive, but you can have an instant landscape.

Taking Care of Your Trees

FERTILIZING TREES

When a plant begins to look ill, whether it's a tree or a philodendron in the house, many people think fertilization is the remedy. Usually a lack of fertilizer is not the problem. If a good lawn fertilization program is being followed, supplemental fertilizer for trees is seldom needed. If a tree is weakened for reasons involving the root system, such as construction damage or poor fill dirt, fertilization may even serve to finish the tree off since all fertilizers are salts and an excess can cause damage. A healthy tree needs considerably more fertilizer than does a tree with damaged roots.

Young trees making nine to twelve inches of terminal growth per year, or large trees making six to nine inches of terminal growth per year, usually are getting sufficient fertilizer. You can check the amount of terminal growth a tree has made in one season by measuring from the tip to the first ring of bud scale scars and from this ring to the next ring of bud scale scars.

How Much Fertilizer?

Fertilizer recommendations are frequently based on the number of inches of trunk diameter. The common recommendation, one pound per inch of trunk diameter, assumes a complete fertilizer such as 12-12-12 is going to be used and that the tree's root system is not confined to a limited area. A more precise way to determine the amount of fertilizer that woody ornamentals need has been suggested by Everett E. Janne and Earl Puls in Texas Agricultural Extension Service bulletin No. L-1097, "Fertilizing Woody Ornamentals." Janne and Puls suggest that fertilizer needs should be based on the number of square feet in the growing area of the branch spread; thus when the root system is restricted by other trees, paved areas or curbs, this is taken into account in computing fertilizer needs. Janne and Puls suggest that the general lawn fertilizer recommendation of 6 pounds of actual nitrogen per 1,000 square feet per

year is satisfactory for tree and shrub care. This amount should be distributed in several applications, beginning with 2 pounds of actual nitrogen per 1,000 square feet in the spring just before new growth starts, with a similar application in the fall about the time of the average date of the first frost. Apply the remaining 2 pounds of nitrogen, in the form of ammonium nitrate, ammonium sulfate or other nitrogen fertilizer, at the rate of ½ to ¾ pound of nitrogen per 1,000 square feet at six- to eight-week intervals through July 30.

Amount of Nitrogen Fertilizers Needed to Supply ½ to 2 lbs. Actual Nitrogen per 1,000 sq. ft.

Material	Approximate pounds of fertilizer needed to supply			
	2 lb. N	1 lb. N	¾ lb. N	½ lb. N
Urea (45-0-0)	4	2	1½	1
Ammonium nitrate (33-0-0)	6	3	2¼	1½
Ammonium sulfate (21-0-0)	10	5	3¾	2½
Complete Fertilizers				
10-10-10	20	10	7½	5
12-12-12	16	8	6	4
10-20-10	20	10	7½	5

Amounts of Phosphorus and Potassium Fertilizer Needed to Supply 3.6 lbs. P$_2$O$_5$ per 1,000 sq. ft. and 6 lbs. Potash (K$_2$O) per 1,000 sq. ft.

Material	Quantity needed per 1,000 sq. ft.	Amount per hole based on 250 holes per 1,000 sq. ft.
Phosphorus (P)		
Superphosphate (0-20-0)	18 lb.	2 tbsp.
Treble superphosphate (0-46-0)	8 lb.	1 tbsp.
Potassium		
Muriate of potash (0-46-0)	10 lb.	1 tbsp.
Nitrogen, phosphorus, potassium		
10-20-10	18 lb.	¼ cup
12-12-12	30 lb.	½ cup

Fertilizer Application

Do not apply fertilizer between July 30 and the average fall frost date because late summer fertilization will stimulate new growth, making the tree more susceptible to winter injury. In tropical regions, of course, this precaution is unnecessary.

For applying nitrogen fertilizers it has been shown that surface application followed by thorough watering (soak the soil to the depth of 6 to 8 inches) is just as efficient at getting the readily soluble nitrogen down to the root system as is the technique of punching or drilling holes to put fertilizer in.

If a complete fertilizer is used, it's good to get the phosphorous and potassium down about 6 inches into the soil. Too often trees are fertilized only in the drip line area, with fertilizer holes punched every 1 to 2 feet apart. Holes for distributing complete fertilizers into the root zone area must be spaced approximately 2 feet apart over the entire root zone area (under the tree's canopy) but not closer than 3 feet from the trunk. Make approximately 250 holes at 2-foot spacings per 1,000 square feet.

Trees and Toadstools

A yard full of brown mushrooms may seem more of a problem than a blessing, but at least as far as trees are concerned, the mushrooms may be helping out. Most woody trees have what are called mycorrhizal fungi which live in association with the tree roots for the mutual benefit of both organisms. Though the mycorrhizal fungus does grow into the plant root tissue, it actually benefits it in several ways. First of all, because the fungal strands also penetrate out into the soil, there is effectively a greater root surface area. Roots infected with mycorrhizal fungi are often more drought- and frost-resistant. There is a higher rate of mineral absorption, especially nitrogen and phosphorous, with mycorrhizal roots. Also, the roots are protected from pathogens because of a fungal mantel which forms a protective mechanical barrier. In addition, the fungus may secrete antibiotics and it may also attract a protective population of other microorganisms, fungi and bacteria. There is some evidence that mycorrhizal roots may be more resistant to root aphids and nematodes, and the roots are protected from soil phytotoxins. The fungus, on the other hand, because of its association with the tree, is better able to compete with other microorganisms. The plant roots supply carbohydrates and are a source of thiamine, other B vitamins and growth factors.

It is quite likely that mycorrhizae have evolved from parasitic fungi to non-lethal varieties through progressive selection. This theory is substantiated by the existence of fungi that form mycorrhizal-like structures on roots which ultimately damage the host. Also, there are fungi which at times live as saprophytes, parasites or

mycorrhizal organisms, depending on environmental circumstances.

Every year, especially in late summer and fall when we receive frequent rains, the Agricultural Extension Service receives many calls from homeowners about numerous large brown toadstools which appear overnight in the lawn. Further

(Continued on next page)

investigation usually reveals that these toadstools almost always occur under ash trees, especially Arizona Ash. There is a particular mycorrhizal fungus (*Gyrodon merulioides*) which only occurs under ash trees and this appears to be the same fungus often reported in the Houston area. It is a large, brown, rather irregular mushroom, and if picked and turned over, it is bright yellow on the other side. These mushrooms are quite prolific and apparently are the fruiting bodies of a mushroom that is aiding the ash tree.

With all these supposed benefits of this type of an association it would only seem obvious that some sort of innoculation of mycorrhizal fungi should be beneficial to many plants. In reality, it rarely has been. In some instances where seedling nurseries have been established in areas void of a particular type of tree and associated mycorrhizae, an innoculation of the seedling or seed bed with mycorrhizal fungi has produced excellent results.

There are many mycorrhizal fungi, however, and in some cases a tree may even be associated with two or more different fungi. Where numerous mycorrhizal fungi exist, innoculation probably is of little benefit. On the other hand, one can't help but wonder if some trees fail or are difficult to transplant because of a lack of suitable mycorrhizae in the soil. For instance, our native "Naked Indian" or Madrone almost always fails in a relatively short time once transplanted out of its area. Much of this may be due to different climates and soil, but it's possible that mycorrhizae could also be involved. In this author's experience at least two trees have failed to grow even though given growing conditions similar to those where they are native. One was an Italian Stone Pine (*Pinus pinea*) and another a Swamp Chestnut Oak (*Quercus prinus*). Neither tree, though given fertilizer and adequate care, has done much more than exist. Perhaps they need some mycorrhizae.

Liquid fertilizer injection is also used to fertilize trees. A high-pressure fertilizer solution is injected into the soil with the aid of a needle or lance. While home-type devices can be used for this, the method is most commonly used in commercial applications to save time because it results in faster uptake of the fertilizer.

Foliar applications of fertilizer are also used, especially for applying minor nutrients such as iron or zinc. Iron chlorosis in trees is symptomized by yellowing of the plant foliage with the leaf veins remaining green. Zinc deficiency also causes a yellowing of plant foliage and is a common problem with pecan and hickory trees.

Foliar materials are effective when sprayed on the foliage in the early spring when new leaves are developing. However, applications of foliar iron may be required later in the season to correct iron chlorosis problems that had been overlooked or not anticipated earlier in the year.

Iron chelate materials can be applied to trees at the rate of 2 level tablespoons per gallon of water for foliar sprays or 2 level tablespoons per diameter inch of tree as a soil application. Soil applications should be mixed with sufficient water to allow even distribution over the root zone area. Iron sulfate can also be used to correct iron chlorosis, at the rate of 5 pounds per 100 gallons of water as a foliar spray (1¼ ounces per gallon). For soil application use ¼ pound per diameter inch of tree. Again, the soil application should be evenly distributed throughout the root zone area.

PRUNING*

Trees growing in the forest rarely get any pruning. When they do it's usually the drastic and detrimental result of a heavy storm, or it occurs as the natural shading out of lower branches in a thick forest. Whenever a tree is wounded, whether accidentally or intentionally, the potential for entry of insects and diseases is greater. The conventional wisdom is that if you paint over wounded areas with an asphalt tree wound dressing, you've given the tree the necessary protection. However, recent research† indicates that insects and diseases get into wounds very soon despite tree wound dressings. This doesn't mean that you shouldn't

---

*Much of the material in this section has been adapted from *Modern Pruning Methods* by A.F. DeWerth, former professor, Dept. of Soil and Crop Sciences, The Texas A&M University System.

---

†Dr. Dan Neely, Plant Pathologist, Illinois Natural History Survey, Urbana, Ill. and Dr. Alex Shigo, Chief Plant Pathologist, U.S. Dept. of Agriculture, Northeastern Forest Experiment Station, Durham, N.H.

prune a tree except to remove dead or diseased limbs; it does mean that a minimum of pruning is probably better than too much. The size of the limbs which are pruned also makes a great difference in the likelihood of infection. Small cuts on limbs less than an inch in diameter heal more quickly and thus are less susceptible to insect or disease damage.

Two big reasons for pruning are (1) to remove dead or diseased limbs and (2) to invigorate trees whose roots may have been damaged during home construction. Pruning is an often overlooked yet very useful way to help these trees recover or, with transplants, to balance the amount of branch growth with the amount of root system at the time of transplanting. Excluding certain fruit trees, few trees are available in bare-root form anymore, but this technique should be used any time, even with container stock, that the root system has to be significantly disturbed.

When trees have been growing in containers too long, it is often necessary to cut and pull the roots out in a more natural manner during planting. Otherwise, they'll continue to spiral around in the form of the container and remain stunted. When this has to be done, obviously some of the roots will be lost and one-third to one-half of the top of the tree will have to be removed.

When to Prune

Trees may be pruned at any time. There are advantages and disadvantages in pruning during certain seasons, but the selection of the time to prune should depend principally on practical considerations.

Trees can be pruned into a desired shape best when they are in foliage. At this time the dead and diseased branches are seen more easily.

Spring is an excellent time for pruning large trees, because rapid healing of wounds occurs at this time. Trees such as maple and birch bleed profusely. They usually are not prevalent in the South but where they are grown, pruning should be done during the summer when they do not bleed as seriously.

Pruning Methods

Regardless of instructions and diagrams given, gardeners will learn more about pruning in their own gardens if they will observe closely each plant, its habit of growth, and its blooming characteristics.

Pay particular attention to the arrangement of the buds because these determine the type of growth that you can expect after pruning.

PRUNING
TOOLS

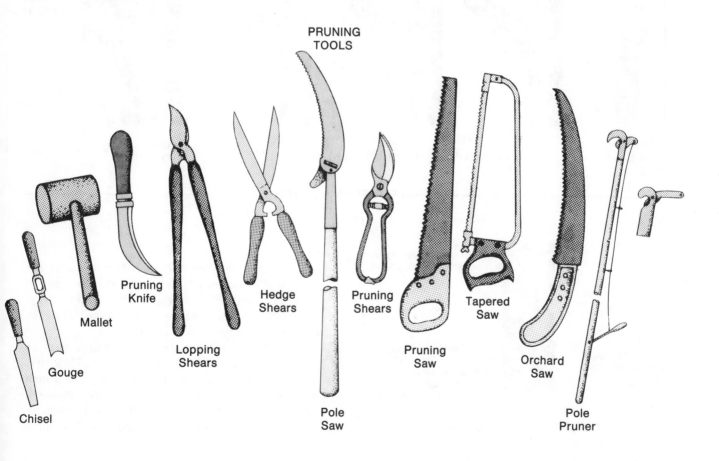

Chisel · Gouge · Mallet · Pruning Knife · Lopping Shears · Hedge Shears · Pole Saw · Pruning Shears · Pruning Saw · Tapered Saw · Orchard Saw · Pole Pruner

Split Limb   Results in Decay

─NO PRUNING─

No Slope in Cut   Results in Decay

─IMPROPER PRUNING─

Bark Peeled   Limb Split

─LIMBS SPLIT FROM IMPROPER PRUNING─

Sloping Cut

Preliminary Cut

Cut to Remove Limb

Start Cut

Final Cut Along Dotted Line

Preliminary Cut Before Removing Stump

Pruning A Small Branch

Pruning A Medium-Size to Large Limb

Removing A Very Large Limb

─PROPER PRUNING METHODS─

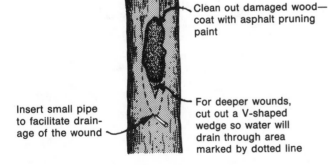

Clean out damaged wood—coat with asphalt pruning paint

Insert small pipe to facilitate drainage of the wound

For deeper wounds, cut out a V-shaped wedge so water will drain through area marked by dotted line

Treating a deep tree wound.

There are two types of bud arrangements on the twigs and branches of trees and shrubs commonly grown in southern landscapes. In a general way, these bud arrangements are largely responsible for the typical growth habit of the plant.

Buds have an alternate or opposite arrangement on the twigs, and most plants will have buds that occur alternately along the stems. A plant which has alternate buds usually will be rounded, pyramidal, inverted pyramidal or columnar in shape. Plants having opposite buds rarely assume any form other than that of a rounded tree or shrub with a rounded crown.

There is no standard method of pruning woody plants. On large shade trees, the most common practice is to start pruning operations in the upper portions of the tree and work downward. It is much easier to shape the tree properly by this method and it also saves time in clearing the pruned branches from the lower portions of the tree, should they become lodged there. Remove dead, broken, insect and fungus-infected branches. Branches that interfere with each other also should be removed. This includes small branches that may become undesirable within a few years.

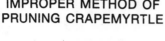

IMPROPER METHOD OF PRUNING CRAPEMYRTLE

PROPER METHOD OF PRUNING CRAPEMYRTLE

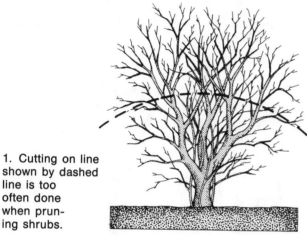

1. Cutting on line shown by dashed line is too often done when pruning shrubs.

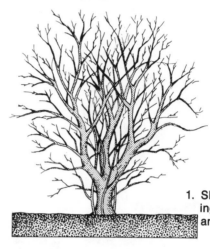

1. Shrub before pruning. Needs all weak and dead branches removed.

2. Same plant after being pruned as indicated above. All sucker growth remains.

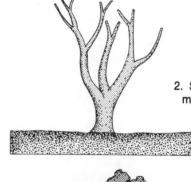

2. Same shrub after removal of weak and interfering branches and with base sucker growth removed.

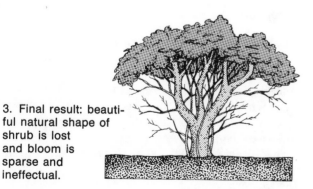

3. Final result: beautiful natural shape of shrub is lost and bloom is sparse and ineffectual.

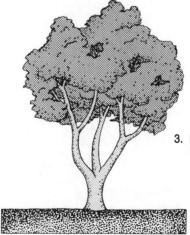

3. Final result: beautiful natural and distinctive form of plant retained. Vigorous growth and prolific and effective flowering.

Pruning Crapemyrties and other multiple-stemmed, low-branching shrubs and trees.

Make clean cuts, as nearly flush as possible with the branch that is to remain. Cut dead branches back to a healthy crotch so that the final cut is surrounded by healthy tissue.

Include the treatment of the bark on the trunk and branches in your pruning operations. Dead bark areas should be cut to healthy tissue and old wounds not healing properly should be recut and shellac and wound dressing should be applied.

Methods for shaping the final cuts and removing large branches are shown on page 20.

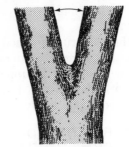
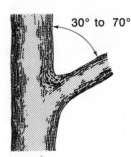

Weak Crotch, Too Narrow

Excellent Angle

30° to 70°

Remove branches that make an angle of less than 30° with the trunk.

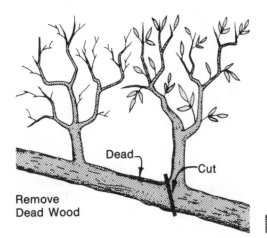

Dead

Cut

Remove Dead Wood

Remove Root Suckers

Remove Water Sprouts

Be sure to prune out all dead wood, root suckers, and water sprouts.

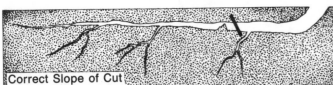
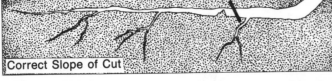

Correct Slope of Cut

Root pruning usually is necessary a year or so before transplanting.

Incorrect Slope of Cut

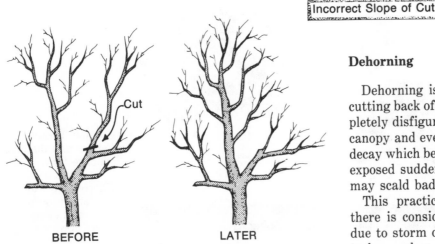

Cut

BEFORE

LATER

Don't allow lateral branches to compete with the main leader.

Dehorning

Dehorning is a practice which involves drastic cutting back of the larger limbs of a tree. This completely disfigures the tree by removing the normal canopy and eventually may lead to serious branch decay which begins at the severed ends. The bark is exposed suddenly to the full rays of the sun and may scald badly.

This practice must be used, however, where there is considerable dying-back of the branches due to storm damage, severe insect or disease attack, or when a reduced root area cannot support such a large canopy. Many detrimental after-effects may be avoided by taking certain precautions. Follow the various cutting practices shown on page 20.

SAFETY RULES FOR PRUNERS

1. Know the type of wood in the tree. Be especially cautious when pruning trees with weak, brittle wood such as silver maple, willow, poplar and tulip. Oak, hickory, pecan, elm and plane trees have strong, flexible wood.

2. Check your pruning tools often for safety and efficiency.

3. Study and decide on the general conditions of the tree. Greater care must be taken in old or weakened trees than in sound ones.

4. If possible, prune when the weather is warm and the trees are dry. When temperatures are low and the trees are wet, the job of pruning is always dangerous. When electric wires run through or near the tree, the danger of electrical shock is increased in wet weather.

5. Never allow tools to come in contact with wires, even though they are supposed to be insulated.

6. Bark peeling and fungus growths are signs of dying and dead branches. Never depend for support on limbs that show these symptoms.

7. When pruning large trees, remember that any branch, no matter how sound in appearance, may give way under the weight of the pruner.

Always have a safety rope properly attached.

PREVENTING DAMAGE TO LANDSCAPE TREES DURING CONSTRUCTION

Some trees just don't like people, especially if those people smother their roots with a foot or more of fill dirt, cut their roots while installing service lines, compact the soil with heavy equipment that excludes even more oxygen from the roots, or change drainage patterns, which eventually alters the water table. They like people even less when, on top of this, they plant a very competitive St. Augustine lawn and fertilize with several hundred pounds of fertilizer salts, not to mention the hundreds of gallons of treated city water dumped on their roots. Older trees, like most older people, are well established and are less tolerant of changes in their environment. When you construct anything on a lot where trees exist, it's important to disturb them as little as possible, both above and below ground. If care isn't taken to insure minimum damage, these trees will often die within several months to several years. Trees damaged during building construction can be adversely affected for years later, and in most cases construction will shorten the life-span of a tree if it doesn't kill it immediately.

Preventing Tree Damage
Due to Fill Soil

When fill soil is placed over an existing root system, it reduces the amount of oxygen available in the original root zone area and may eventually suffocate the roots. Dying roots are unable to pick up water or fertilizer elements, and above-ground symptoms are soon noticeable in the tree. By the

The fill soil and pavement placed over this tree's root zone have begun to kill the tree. Note the sparse foliation and dying growth, particularly at the center-right portion of the tree.

time these symptoms become severe it's usually too late to do much about the problem. So, if you know that fill dirt will be needed around the tree, it is possible to prevent some of this damage with proper treatment. Since these treatments are costly, it is important to determine which trees are worth this additional expense required to save them.

Consider the number of trees that exist on the lot and the importance of the location of any that may be affected by fill dirt. If you have a great many trees that won't have to be covered with fill dirt, and if the trees that will be covered are not vital to your home landscape, it's best to sacrifice these rather than going to the expense of fill damage prevention.

The species and variety of tree that will be affected by the fill dirt is also important. Some trees simply aren't worth the extra cost and trouble of damage prevention; long-lived trees such as many of the oaks, on the other hand, are probably worth saving.

Again, it's the larger trees, which are more set in their ways, that are likely to be severely damaged by fill dirt and associated construction damage problems. Younger trees are more vigorous and more tolerant of small amounts of fill dirt and other types of construction damage.

Installing 12 Inches or More of Fill Dirt Around Existing Trees

Begin by removing all vegetation including sod and underbrush in the root zone area (a tree's root zone area extends approximately three feet from the trunk out to the edge of the branches and slightly beyond). If left under a layer of fill dirt, the vegetation begins to decompose, and, because there is a shortage of oxygen in this area, the resultant products of decomposition are toxic and may damage the tree roots.

Fertilizer can then be applied over the root zone area prior to installation of the fill (see section on Fertilizing Trees, page 17). To prevent soil or other fill material from coming in direct contact with the tree trunk, a dry well should be constructed using brick, rock, railroad ties or other material which will keep the fill at least 1 to 2 feet from the trunk.

A wagon wheel design using 4-inch agricultural clay clay tile or 4-inch perforated PVC pipe arranged in five or six horizontal lines radiating from the tree well and attached by circular wheel design at a point just beyond the branch spread is then laid out. To provide ventilation to this tile system, four to six-inch bell tile is placed upright over the

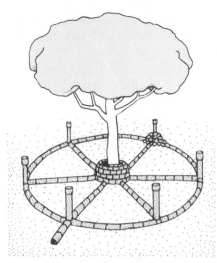

Drainage tile installation with a dry well and vertical bell tile provide aeration for tree roots beneath deep soil fill.

junction of the radial lines with the circle. These upright tiles should extend to the surface of the planned grade level so that air will be able to filter down through them readily. The low end of the wagon wheel should be drained off with additional tile to a curb or other drainage reservoir.

The wagon wheel design is then covered with coarse rock or gravel to a depth of 6 to 18 inches, followed with a layer of finer gravel. Soil can be prevented from filtering into the gravel with a covering of straw, hay or other porous material. The plastic shade cloth material often used for greenhouses will also make an excellent long-lasting filter to prevent soil from washing down into the gravel.

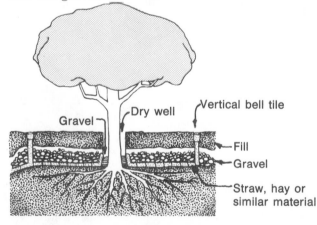

Cross section of a completed soil fill around an established tree. Soil fill is placed over a ventilating tile system.

If it is necessary to fill the tree well to keep from having an open hole, a coarse material such as gravel or coarse pine bark should be used. This serves a dual purpose, for it will keep rodents from entering the tile system. A similar material can also be placed in the upright bell tile and covered with a screen or grill to prevent rodents from making nests in the tile system.

Preventing Damage When Installing Less Than Twelve Inches of Fill Dirt

In many instances it's necessary to use more fill dirt than the tree can adjust to but not enough to fit the tile and gravel underneath. In this instance, instead of tile, put down a layer of coarse gravel for the majority of the fill. Sod and underbrush still must be removed and fertilizer applied if necessary. This gravel layer should be tapered upward toward the base of the tree, where it may be 8 to 12 inches deep. Out at the extremeties of the branches, the fill gravel may be as shallow as 3 to 6 inches. Some material such as that discussed on page 24 should be used to prevent soil from filtering into the gravel and before a layer of soil is placed over the top of this gravel. It is important in all instances to use a good quality, loose fill soil.

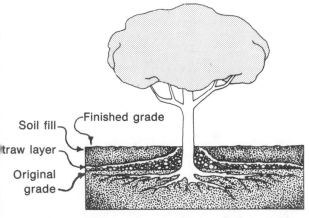

Coarse gravel placed over the original grade will provide aeration for tree roots beneath shallow soil zone.

Preventing Tree Damage When Lowering an Existing Grade

There is usually less danger of damaging a tree when removing soil than there is when adding soil. Where large cuts in grade are made it is a good idea to construct terraces or retaining walls to avoid excessive loss of soil from these cuts, but where only 1 to 2 inches of soil are removed, and care is taken to water thoroughly during dry periods and avoid damage from drought, most trees will be little affected by this type of soil removal. Since some of the roots will be damaged, it is important that the trees be pruned to thin out the branch spread and compensate for root loss. It may be necessary to

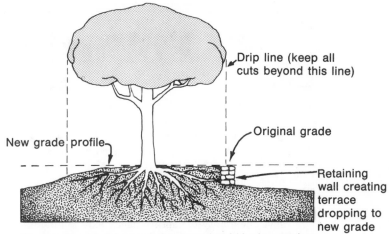

The grade around an existing tree should be lowered as illustrated. A terrace or retaining wall can be used to prevent excessive soil loss.

remove as much as ⅓ to ½ of the total branch area in order to compensate for damaged roots. If large roots have been cut, make sure that the cuts are trimmed up rather than left ragged and torn, and painting with a pruning paint or tree wound dressing may help to prevent entrance of wood-rotting fungi.

Saving Trees After Fill Dirt Has Already Begun to Cause Damage

This is one of the most frustating situations for both tree owner and arborist. An arborist can't offer you any type of guarantee, the treatment may be rather expensive, and the trees often die anyway. Unfortunately, to date little has been done to resolve the problem. Most often the treatment offered by arborists is to pump some miracle ingredient into the soil which will save the trees. Since oxygen loss is the problem—and there's no liquid substitute for oxygen—unless someone comes up with an easy way of reintroducing oxygen into the soil, treatment for trees damaged under these circumstances will continue to be expensive and hope for recovery slim.

Many techniques have been tried. Usually a lawn is already established, and most people don't want to remove the entire soil covering. Attempts have been made to drill holes with a soil auger at 2-foot intervals throughout the root zone area and fill these with gravel perforated plastic pipe filled with gravel to allow air passages back to the existing soil line. In some parts of the country high-pressure air fracturing is used to open cavities in the fill soil which are then filled in with a coarse

Pollution Damage to Trees*

Today there is considerable interest in pollution and the effect it has on plant materials as well as people. Not only are plants affected by pollution, but, to a certain extent, they have the ability to filter out and detoxify some of the pollutants which might otherwise affect man. It has been shown, for example, that leaf hairs (trichomes) have the ability to capture particulate pollutants from the air and can detoxify many gases such as sulfur dioxide provided the pollutants are not present in concentration great enough to damage the leaf. Some trees which have been shown to have resistance to air pollutants in the South are:

Scientific Name	Common Name
Acacia berlandieri	Berlandier Acacia
Acacia farnesiana	Sweet Acacia
Broussonetia papyrifera	Common Papermulberry
Ilex aquifolium	English Holly
Ilex opaca	American Holly
Koelreuteria apiculata	Goldenraintree
Koelreuteria paniculata	Panicled Goldenraintree
Melia azedarach	Chinaberry
Phoenix canariensis	Canary Island Date
Phoenix dactylifera	Date
Phoenix reclinata	Senegral Date
Quercus virginiana	Live Oak

AIR POLLUTANTS THAT DAMAGE TREES

Pollutants	Sources	Symptoms	Age of leaves affected
Sulfur dioxide (SO₂)	One of the primary sources is the combustion of coal and petroleum products; it is also an impurity which may be released during the refining of a number of metals.	*Broadleaved trees:* Burned areas which turn yellow, tan or ivory between the veins. *Conifers:* Needles turn yellow or brown, sometimes in a banding pattern.	Leaves which have recently become mature.
Ozone	The natural source is electrical storms, but this only rarely causes plant damage and probably never causes significant damage to trees. The problem source occurs during a reaction with sunlight and nitrogen oxides plus hydrocarbons released during the burning of petroleum fuels.	*Broadleaved trees:* Stippling of the upper leaf surface. Color of these necrotic areas varies from white to brown; leaves may develop purplish pigmentation.	Leaves which are recently mature.
Hydrogen fluoride (HF)	Only very small quantities of hydrogen fluoride, often parts per billion, are required to damage sensitive plants. It is produced when such products as aluminum, steel, brick, tile, ceramics, pottery, glass, phosphate fertilizers, cement and fiber glass are manufactured, and it is also an impurity produced in the combustion of coal.	*Broadleaved trees:* The tips and marginal areas of leaves are first affected because the fluoride accumulates in these areas. Ultimately, a dark reddish brown area develops along the margins and tips of the leaves. *Conifers:* Reddish brown tip burn of needles some dwarfing and droppage of needles may occur. Pines are often rather sensitive.	Fully mature leaves and new needles on pines.
Chlorine (Cl₂)	Chlorine is primarily a problem from leakage, however, burning of insulation or plastic may also release significant amounts of chlorine.	*Broadleaved trees:* Leaf yellowing and severe damage may appear very similar to that caused by ozone.	Newly matured leaves; with older and then younger leaves less susceptible.
Peroxyacetyl nitrate (PAN)	This is another pollutant which occurs in the presence of sunlight and is dependent on nitrogen oxides and hydrocarbons.	*Broadleaved trees:* Damage from this pollutant occurs primarily on the underside of the leaf and bronzing is usually apparent. *Conifers:* Yellowing of needles and heavy needle drop.	Young.
Ammonia (NH₃)	Ammonia, like chlorine, is often a result of spillage.	*Broadleaved trees:* Leaf tissue is quickly burned by ammonia gas and may turn light yellow and in many instances develop purple or bronzed areas between the leaf veins. Flowers are often unaffected and most plants and trees will recover quickly because of the fertilization effect and may make more growth than normal during the year. *Conifers:* Conifers are much less affected, but if the damage is acute, the needles may turn brown or black.	All leaves are usually affected, however, the very new growth in many species seems to be more resistant.
Smoke, dust and other particles in the air	Combustion of petroleum, burning of trash, cement production, and other industrial incineration.	Obvious coating on the leaves which causes a general loss in vigor and hardiness.	All leaves.

*Adapted from A.F. DeWerth, former professor, Dept. of Soil and Crop Sciences, The Texas A&M University System.

(Continued from page 25)

gravel. Any ingenious technique you can think of to increase oxygen content in the original soil area may work. In most cases, however, it will be necessary to remove the soil around the tree trunk down to the original soil level for a radius of at least 2 feet from the trunk. A dry well is then installed around the trunk to hold the soil in place. Holes can be dug with a post hole digger every 2 feet at the drip line, and these can be filled with coarse gravel; a 4-inch perforated plastic pipe filled with coarse gravel may be more permanent since gravel alone will eventually fill in with soil parts.

Deeper fills will require additional aeration. Again, the soil should be removed at the base of the tree, but in this case it's necessary to use radial trenches. Small trenching machines can be rented for digging gradually sloping trenches to the outer root zone area at approximately the original soil line. A circular trench must also be dug under the drip line connecting these radial arms, similar to

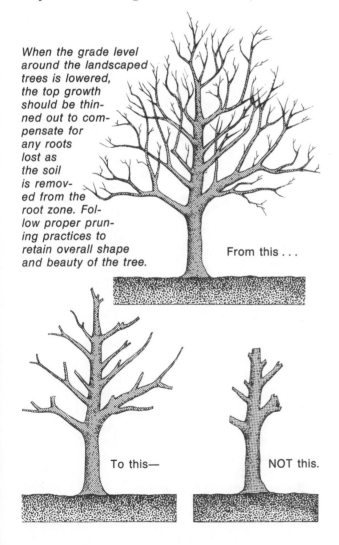

When the grade level around the landscaped trees is lowered, the top growth should be thinned out to compensate for any roots lost as the soil is removed from the root zone. Follow proper pruning practices to retain overall shape and beauty of the tree.

From this . . .

To this—

NOT this.

the system installed prior to applying large amounts of fill (see page 24). This tile should then be covered with coarse gravel, and some material such as plastic shade cloth should be used to prevent soil sifting in over the tile. In either case it is particularly important to prune the trees back one-third to one-half to compensate for what has already been a loss of root system and, hopefully, to invogorate the tree. At this stage, because the tree's root system has been severely damaged, additional fertilizer, except perhaps small amounts of phosphorous, may be undesirable.

PROPAGATING TREES FROM SEED*

Trees for use in home landscapes are rarely propagated from seed, although this is possible. Most seeds, especially those from trees which are not of tropical origin, have some dormancy requirement prior to germination. Some tree seeds may be so hard that they physically prevent expansion of the embryo, or they may prevent entry of oxygen and water to the developing embryo. In this case, scarifying the seed coat with a file or pouring boiling water on the seeds and allowing them to cool may soften the seed coat sufficiently. Many seeds, however, may require stratification, a cold, moist treatment.

These germination requirements are often necessary for survival, for if tree seeds that mature in the fall germinated immediately, the tiny seedlings probably would be killed by frost. Most tree seeds produced in the fall can be germinated either by planting in the fall or by storing in damp peat moss wrapped in a plastic bag for approximately 90 days, after which they can be planted in flats in a sunny window or in a greenhouse. Extremely hard seeds, such as redbud seed, should be scarified prior to this treatment; other seeds, such as magnolia seed, which have an oily, red aril (seed coat), are best cleaned prior to stratification.

Treatments for Hard to Germinate Seed

Three methods are commonly used to treat seedcoats that cannot be penetrated by water. Soaking in sulphuric acid; soaking in hot water or dipping for a very short period of time in boiling water; and mechanical scarification or nicking.

---

*Much of the material in this section has been adapted from *The Propagation of Ornamental Plants* by A.F. DeWerth, former professor, Dept. of Soil and Crop Sciences, The Texas A&M University System.

PROPAGATION BY GRAFTING

Grafting is an ancient and fascinating form of plant propagation. This is a horticultural practice in which a short piece of stem bearing one or more growth buds taken from one plant is inserted into another plant to form a union.

When a graft is successful and the branch grows from it, it produces flowers and fruits like the plant from which the stem piece was taken. The remainder of the plant below will continue to produce the same flowers and fruits as before.

An individual who becomes interested in grafting must understand well three terms fundamental to the process. These words are: *stock*, *scion*, and *cambium*. *Stock* is used to indicate the plant upon which the graft is made. *Scion* is the piece of stem containing one or more growth buds that is inserted into the stock. *Cambium* is the soft layer of tissue in a stem that lies between the bark and the wood. Through cell division, this layer has the capacity to produce new bark tissue on the outside and wood tissue on the inside.

The basic principle in grafting is to join a section of the cambium layer of the scion with the cambium layer of the stock as completely as possible and to bind the stock and scion together so that a union takes place between the two cambium layers.

The various types of grafts that can be made are shown in the illustrations. In all grafting methods,

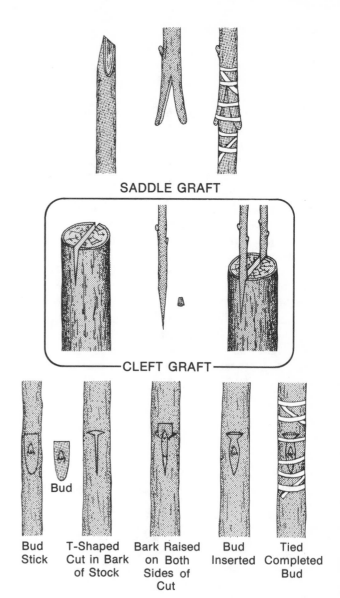

SADDLE GRAFT

CLEFT GRAFT

| Bud Stick | T-Shaped Cut in Bark of Stock | Bark Raised on Both Sides of Cut | Bud Inserted | Tied Completed Bud |

Bud

BUD GRAFTING OR BUDDING

the tight union between stock and scion must be sealed off from the air with some type of sealing agent. The best method for the amateur is to use a manufactured water base asphalt emulsion that comes in small cans.

Plants used for stock and scion must have a close botanical relationship, but even some closely related species and varieties are not compatible.

Deciduous trees and shrubs can be grafted any time during the dormant season. In most cases it is most satisfactory if it is done before buds begin to swell in late winter or early spring. Most evergreens can be grafted in early spring before active growth begins.

Root grafting can be done also by using pieces of roots made in the same manner as described for making root cuttings, except, the pieces should be

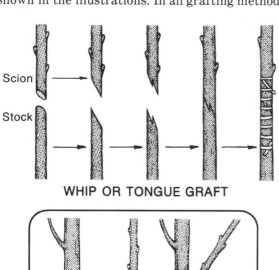

Scion

Stock

WHIP OR TONGUE GRAFT

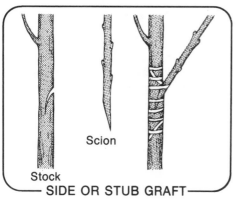

Scion

Stock

SIDE OR STUB GRAFT

made with a straight cut across the root on the end nearest the parent plant and a slanting cut on the end farthest from the parent plant. Cut a scion in the same manner. Then make a splice graft and handle the grafts in the same manner that root cuttings are planted.

PROPAGATION BY BUDDING

Budding is a type of grafting that is performed with a scion that has only one growth bud. The bud from one plant is inserted under the bark of a closely related plant. If this is done properly, and the two plants are compatible, the bud and the stock will unite. Budding is usually done in the summer and early fall with most plants since through the fall and winter the growth bud remains dormant. In the spring when active growth begins in all buds of the plant, the inserted bud also starts to grow, and the branch just above it can be cut off. Then all the growth from this bud will be identical to the plant from which the bud was taken.

While the results of budding are the same as those accomplished by any other type of grafting, it is much easier to accomplish for several reasons.

Buds can be placed in the bottom 3 or 4 inches of a seedling or a rooted cutting. If the bud does not take, the plant is not disfigured as it would be with an unsuccessful graft. An undesirable plant can be converted into a better variety, or another variety could be added to an established plant.

The plant or the section of the plant into which the bud is placed is called the stock. In budding, a branch or a firm round twig with several buds and a diameter slightly smaller than a pencil is cut from the desired plant. The leaves are cut from a portion of branch with a very sharp knife leaving only a short piece of each petiole below each bud for easy handling. This branch from which the buds will be taken before they are inserted is called a *budstick*. The budsticks must be kept fresh and firm. After they are prepared they are usually carried in a small box or moist sphagnum moss to prevent their drying.

When a bud is to be inserted into the upper branches of an older shrub or large tree choose a branch 1 or 2 years old, remove the foliage that might interfere with the budding operation and proceed as shown in the illustration.

Patch budding is used, however, on plants that have a thick bark such as avocado, walnut or pecan. Double-bladed tools are available that remove about a 1-inch long rectangle of bark. A patch of bark must peel freely if a patch bud is to be made. In using this method, it is essential to work rapidly so that the tissues do not dry out. The newly inserted patch must be held securely in place by rubber strips or waxed cloth, and all cuts must be carefully covered.

The present practice is to use rubber budding strips or soft, rubber budding patches to tie the buds. These materials exert an even pressure without cutting the plant, and they do not require as much attention as other binding materials. In most cases they do not have to be cut, since they deteriorate and fall from the plant in a short time.

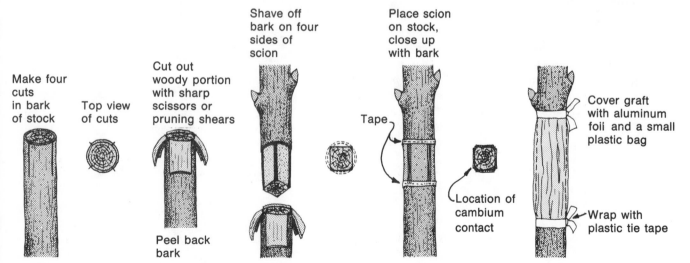

Make four cuts in bark of stock

Top view of cuts

Cut out woody portion with sharp scissors or pruning shears

Peel back bark

Shave off bark on four sides of scion

Place scion on stock, close up with bark

Tape

Location of cambium contact

Cover graft with aluminum foil and a small plastic bag

Wrap with plastic tie tape

"Banana" grafting is a simple, effective way to graft smaller stocks and scions (¼ to ½ inch in diameter).

Tree Pests

Pine Bark Beetles

Pine bark beetles kill more southern pines than do any other insects or diseases. There are five species of pine bark beetles that attack southern pines. They spend most of their lives underneath the bark of their host trees, where the adult beetles chew out the galleries. The young larvae also chew galleries, and when fully developed they pupate, become adult beetles, and chew through the bark to fly and attack other trees. The tree dies because the conductive tissue has been girdled by the

Bark Beetle

feeding or tunneling of these insects. Pine bark beetles are small insects, most are less than ¼ inch long, and they make entry holes about the size of a pencil lead. Other signs of attack are the reddish-brown boaring dust in the bark crevices and around the base of the tree and small masses of pine resin, called pitch tubes, which are usually scattered over the bark surface. In latter stages of attack heavily infested trees begin to die rapidly, with the needles discoloring near the top of the tree. The condition rapidly progresses over the entire tree crown.

Pine bark beetles seem to prefer trees which are already weakened due to construction damage, etc., so those high-value ornamental pines in residential areas are often susceptible. Anything that helps keep the tree as vigorous as possible is advised. Watering during dry periods will help, fertilizer will help if the tree's root system has not been severely damaged, and when the trees are weak or if you know that pine bark beetles are actively working in your area, protecting the trees by spraying with chemicals is advisable. Spray the main trunk, from the ground line to the first

branches, with BHC or lindane. The spray should be applied until the solution begins to run down the bark crevices. Begin spraying at the uppermost point and work to the base of the tree.

Small home sprayers often are incapable of applying an adequate amount of spray to the top of the tree, so it may be necessary to hire professional pest control specialists to do the job. Be sure to get *professional* help and avoid hiring door-to-door so-called "tree specialists." At present, no systemic insecticide applied to the soil is labeled for use in control of pine bark beetles or borers.

Borers

Shade tree borers usually attack hardwood species but may attack pine trees too. They are generally not as devastating as the southern pine beetle, and they, too, prefer to attack weakened trees. Most of these borers are either flat-headed or round-headed. The flat-headed primarily attack newly transplanted shade trees and are generally less destructive than the round-headed borers.

Round-headed borers typically burrow into the hardwood, tunneling holes as large or larger than a pencil. The borers entrance usually contains a sawdust-like residue and often there is a discharge of sap from the tunnel opening which discolors the tree's bark below the boring.

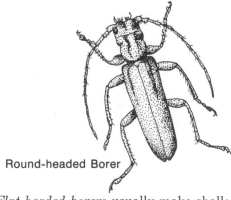

Round-headed Borer

Flat-headed borers usually make shallow, long-winding galleries beneath the bark on the sunny side of the tree. Tunnels made by the larvae of flat-headed borers do not have outside exit holes, although sawdust-like frass may be seen in the cracks of the bark.

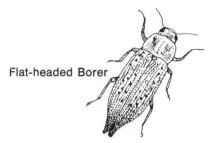

Flat-headed Borer

Sap suckers, which are not borers but are actually small birds related to woodpeckers, sometimes damage trees. They leave regular rows of holes circling the trunk or larger limbs of the tree. Sapsuckers do very little damage, and it is difficult to control them anyway.

Prevention of Borers

Wrapping newly planted trees with aluminum or special nursery wrapping paper will help prevent borers in young trees. Spraying with BHC or lindane is also good for young or weak trees. Watering and fertilizing trees to maintain vigorous growth is important, as is pruning any dead or dying branches and treating wounds with a tree wound dressing. Some species of trees, such as the Arizona Ash, are so susceptible to borer attack that spraying may be the only way to prevent infestation.

Controlling Borers Already in the Trees

Once borers get into the wood of a tree, control is very difficult. Sometimes the holes where the borers have gone in can be located, cleaned out with a wire, and then treated by injecting carbon disulfide, ethylene dichloride or paradichlorobenzene into each tunnel. Spraying into these tunnels with either lindane of BHC and plugging the entrances back up with mud or putty will also provide some control.

Twig Girdlers

Twig girdlers are also borers, but the type of damage they do is considerably different. They damage trees and shrubs by pruning off the limbs. The female does the pruning as she lays eggs on a portion of the limb which eventually breaks off. Twig girdlers especially like Mimosa trees but they also attack Huisache, Pecan, Persimmon, Hickory, Poplar and other shade trees. Because they have a number of wild hosts it's very difficult to control them on home trees. Girdling damage begins during late summer and is usually not noticeable until fall, when the twigs begin to drop to the ground.

Spraying with malathion or carbaryl in mid August and again in late August may help control this pest. Since it is only laying eggs at this time and not feeding on the damaged portion of the tree, they are difficult to control chemically. If the severed twigs are gathered and destroyed, the population of the insect can be reduced since the twigs contain eggs and larvae from last year's generation.

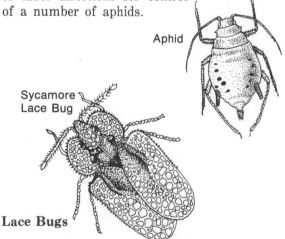

Twig Girdler

Aphids (Plant Lice)

Aphids are small pear-shaped insects that suck the juices out of plants. They attack many plants, including trees. As they feed they excrete a honeydew on which a black, sooty mold often develops. In addition, some aphids may cause galls (swollen, abnormal growths on the leaves, twigs or seed). Problems with aphids depend on a number of things, chief among which are the weather and a build-up of predator insects. If not checked during certain years when they develop in large numbers, they may cause severe damage to trees. Most aphids are relatively easy to control, and chemicals such as diazinon, dimethoate, malathion, metasystox-R, and dormant oil may be used according to label directions for control of a number of aphids.

Aphid

Sycamore Lace Bug

Lace Bugs

Lace bugs are also sucking insects. They are particularly fond of sycamore and sweetgum trees, inflicting damage to aphids, and can be controlled with many of the same chemicals.

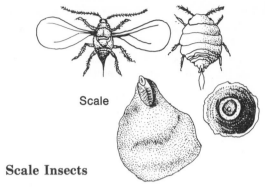

Scale

Scale Insects

Scale insects destroy many trees. Some of the wax scales, in particular, seem to have built up noticeably in the Houston area since 1971. They excrete large quantities of honeydew, on which a black, sooty mildew grows densely. Scale insects can often be controlled by applying a dormant oil, but control during the growing season requires the use of an insecticide such as malathion, diazinon or dimethoate. It is very important to make three or four applications of the insecticide at 7- to 10-day intervals to control nymphs emerging from previously lain eggs.

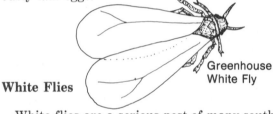

Greenhouse White Fly

White Flies

White flies are a serious pest of many southern shade trees. The adult fly most often observed doesn't do any damage, but the immature stage is a sucking insect. Like aphids and other sucking insects they excrete a sticky honeydew on which you get a black, sooty growth. White flies are not easily controlled, but a dormant oil or a summer oil plus an insecticide may do the job. Insecticides such as diazinon, dimethoate, endosulfan, lindane, malathion, meta-systox-R and naled will control white flies. Be sure to observe all label recommendations before applying any of these materials.

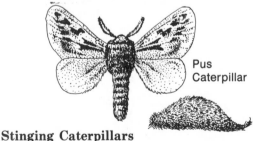

Pus Caterpillar

Stinging Caterpillars

There are a number of stinging caterpillars, including the so-called "asp" (puss caterpillar), which are common in the South and often attack our southern shade trees. The damage they do may not be extensive, but coming in contact with one of these larvae may be a very painful experience. Another rather beautiful stinging caterpillar is the IO moth; the Saddleback caterpillar or Hagg moth may sometimes be found on southern shade trees. These pests are most numerous in late summer and fall and should be controlled as soon as possible. They are rather easy to control with insecticides; carbaryl (sevin) does a good job, and the biological spray *Bacillus thuringiensis* will control several of these pests.

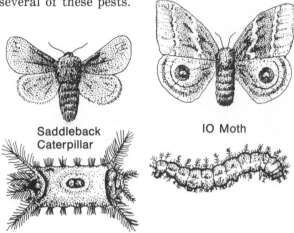

Saddleback Caterpillar   **IO Moth**

Web Worms and Tent Caterpillars

Both the fall web worm and the tent caterpillar are often seen defoliating trees in the South. The regular tent caterpillar and the fall web worm both make webs. The former makes webs mainly in the small limb crotches; the fall web worm produces a large web over clusters of leaves. One species of tent caterpillar, the forest tent caterpillar, generally does not make webs but can be seen in large numbers chewing leaves in the trees. These pests are relatively easily controlled with carbaryl, and they may also be susceptible to *Bacillus thuringiensis*. The latter material should be applied in the evening since it is sensitive to ultra-violet and, in addition, the insects do much of their feeding in the evening and will eat this material, become sick and eventually die. Small concentrations of web worms within reach are often burned as a means of control.

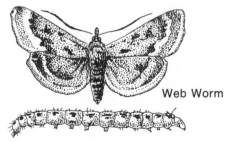

Web Worm

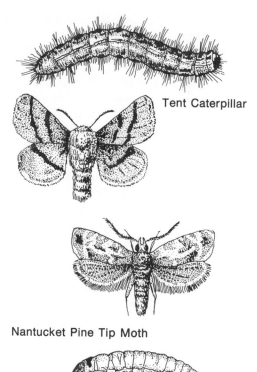

Tent Caterpillar

Nantucket Pine Tip Moth

Nantucket Pine Tip Moth

The pine tip moth is a serious pest of the loblolly pine, a common pine in the South. One of the best remedies for this pest is to plant slash pine, which is less susceptible. Insecticidal control is possible but really isn't practical except for extremely valuable trees or those which are small enough to make spraying feasible. Carbaryl and malathion will control these pests, but it's necessary to make applications April 1, June 1, July 15 and September 1. The cost of spraying a large pine tree makes it rather evident that this type of control is not commonly practiced.

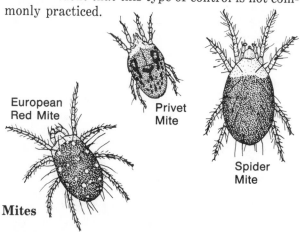

European Red Mite

Privet Mite

Spider Mite

Mites

There are a number of mites which attack southern trees. They are very small and are best observed with a small hand lens or dissecting microscope. Sycamore and Arborvitae are par-

ticularly susceptible and for this and a number of other reasons these two plant species are not recommended for planting in the South. Control is difficult, but the use of kelthane once a week for three applications should provide satisfactory control in most cases.

Phytotoxicity

Phytotoxicity is characterized as damage to the plant foliage, usually in the form of marginal leaf burn, chlorosis or spotting. Distortion or abnormal growth may also be a symptom of plants damaged by a pesticide. Although any portion of the plant may be damaged, the new growth is the most likely to be hurt. Plant damage from pesticides can be minimized by spraying during the cooler portion of the day. Applications should be made either in the early morning or in the late evening. Wettable powders are generally less likely to burn than emulsifiable concentrate sprays but, of course, wettable powders leave an objectionable residue on the foliage.

Shade Tree Diseases

Most shade tree diseases are of little consequence unless something else is also reducing the tree's vigor. Trees will almost always have some minor disease problem such as a leaf-spotting fungus or perhaps a small amount of wood rot, and there is the potential in many species for very damaging diseases that occur even without any weakening caused by construction or other human or environmental causes. Some serious shade tree diseases are described below.

Root Rot. Root rot comes in a number of forms but it is generally caused by a fungus. Particularly damaging are cotton root rot and mushroom root rot. These organisms can be severe on trees even that would otherwise be growing vigorously, however, they are often a primary problem on trees growing out of their natural range or in areas where poor drainage is at fault. Unfortunately, even if you are certain that a tree has root rot there is very little if anything that you can do to effectively control this disease except to remedy any related problems, such as poor drainage, which may be prompting it. Pruning the trees to thin out the foliage load on the root system may also be an invigorating factor as well as fertilization with nitrogen fertilizers in some cases. If you don't know the answer to a tree's problem it's very tempting and easy to blame it on root rot. If you're unscrupulous then it's also very easy to come up with some magical formula to pump into the ground which will control it.

Wood Rot. The trunk and limbs of the tree may also be attacked by various fungi, though not the same ones that attack the root system. These organisms generally enter the tree through wounds or improperly pruned branches. Unless the infection is severe, the tree may remain quite healthy though possibly weakened structurally. There is no control except to use care in treating wounds and in pruning to avoid initial infection.

Slime Flux. Slime flux is particularly severe on elm trees but may attack other trees as well. It is characterized by a bleeding of sap which simply will not dry up. The disease is caused by a bacterium which lives and multiplies in the tree's conductive system. This organism generates considerable pressure, which forces the sap out through wounds in the tree. Because of this constant flow the area is not allowed to heal. If the pressure can be relieved by drilling holes into the infected area and inserting ½-inch galvanized pipe into the hole, it may be possible to dry up the slime flux. In some cases several tubes may be necessary. Be sure to drill the holes or an upward slope so that the sap will flow down.

Iron Chlorosis*

Iron chlorosis is a condition which results when the green chlorophyll in plants fails to develop or is destroyed. The chlorosis normally appears first on young leaves. The leaves of chlorotic plants range from light green to yellow to almost white, usually accompanied by striping. Most soils on which iron chlorosis occurs contain iron which is unavailable to plants, usually the result of alkalinity.

Other Types of Chlorosis. Chlorosis or yellowing of plants can result from poor soil aeration and nitrogen deficiency. However, under these conditions the lower leaves are affected first. Virus diseases also may cause a chlorosis similar to iron deficiency. These disease symptoms are different in that the leaf veins first become yellow with the whole leaf eventually turning yellow.

---

*Adapted from "Iron Chlorosis," a bulletin by C.D. Welch and Carl Gray, Extension Soil Chemists, The Texas A&M University System.

Prevention and Control. Iron chlorosis prevention calls for treatment of soil so that iron becomes available. Application of large amounts of well-rotted organic material on a regular basis tends to make the soils less alkaline and the iron more available. Well-decomposed compost plus 1 pound of powdered sulfur per 100 square feet can be used to make the soil less alkaline. Acid peat also can be used.

To control chlorosis by the addition of iron, use iron sulfate (copperas) or iron chelates according to instructions in the table. Iron sulfate is generally best for spray applications. Chelates are preferred for soil treatments.

Iron chelates are organic compounds which can hold iron in an available form for plant use. A chelating compound acts in much the same way as a crab's claw encloses an object. Chelates can be mixed in the soil. They remain available longer than iron sulfate and normally are needed in smaller quantities for soil applications.

Rates listed in the table will vary with conditions and types of iron chelates. Check the container for iron concentration in the chelate to be used. If the chelate is in solution to be diluted, rates of application should be based on the final concentration.

Method of Application. Before iron compounds are applied, be sure that the observed chlorosis is iron deficiency. For trees, soil application is more effective if placed in holes punched with a crow bar or similar tool to a depth of about 2 feet. The holes should be even with the outer edge of the spread of the branches for trees or in the area of small feeder roots. The holes for shrubs should be 1 to 3 feet from the plants depending on size. For flowers, band the iron sulfate 2 to 3 inches to the side, and 4 to 6 inches below the seed or young plant.

Spray applications of both sulfates and chelates should take place in the late evening when the plant is actively growing. Late evening applications result in less evaporation, thus reducing the danger of burning. When preparing the spray solutions, add 1 teaspoon of soap detergent for each gallon of water for better coverage of foliage.

Spray applications generally give quicker results than soil applications. However, the effect will normally not be as long-lasting and repeat applications may be necessary. Sometimes three to four applications at 2- to 3-week intervals are necessary to control the chlorosis. A combination soil treatment and spray application may give best results. Applying iron on the leaves usually reduces the

Suggested Rates of Iron Chelate and Iron Sulfate

Plant	Iron chelate (dry)[1]		Iron sulfate	
	Foliar spray	Soil application	Foliar spray	Soil application
Lawn and turf grasses	3 level tbs. gal. water. Wet leaves thoroughly.	1 lb. per 1,000 sq. ft.	4 level tbs. per gal. water. Wet leaves thoroughly. (repeat)	10 lbs. per 1,000 sq. ft.
Ornamentals[2]	1 level tbs. per gal. water. Wet plants thoroughly.	2 level tbs. per plant.	3 level tbs. per gal. water. Wet plants thoroughly.	½ lb. per 100 sq. ft. (repeat if necessary).
Fruit trees	2 level tbs. per gal. water. Wet leaves thoroughly.	2 level tbs. per diameter in. of tree.	5 lbs. per 100 gal. water. Wet leaves thoroughly.	¼ lb. per diameter in. of tree.
Vegetables	2 level tbs. per gal. water. Wet plants thoroughly.	1 lb. per 1,000 sq. ft. before planting.	3 level tbs. per gal. water. Wet foliage thoroughly.	5 lbs. per 1,000 sq. ft. and mix with soil.

[1]These rates are based on chelates containing from 8 to 10 percent iron. If the product used is in solution or of a different concentration, adjust the suggested rates up or down to give comparable amounts of iron.

[2]Ornamentals include trees, flowers and shrubs. Spray applications should be accompanied by soil applications of iron. These can be applied as a spray on the soil at the time plants are sprayed.

chlorosis within 5 to 7 days. Soil treatments require longer to be effective but last longer.

Iron sulfate (copperas) will stain concrete and light colored brick. Therefore, careful control of both spray and granular applications is needed to prevent damage.

Mistletoe

Mistletoe is a parasitic plant which invades the tree limbs and may eventually become so prevalent throughout the tree structure that it not only makes the tree look bad but also ruins its health. The only control for mistletoe is to physcially prune it out.

Ball Moss

Spanish Moss, symbol of the South, is usually not controlled, but a close relative, ball moss may actually damage the trees by constricting the small limbs, especially in more western areas of the South. These plants are not parasitic on the trees, but they do attach themselves to the tree. They can be controlled by the use of a copper fungicide. These materials are most effective when applied soon after a rainy period; two applications generally are necessary.

Lichens

Lichens frequently appear on tree trunks in humid areas, and while they may have an unkempt appearance, they do not attack the tree. This occurence on trees may be an indication of poor health. If desired, they may be controlled by using a copper fungicide.

Fungal Leaf Spots

Most of the fungus organisms that cause leaf spotting on trees are of minor importance unless the tree is already weakened. Since diseases need to be prevented, if you know that a tree is weak or if you've had brown leaf spot problems with it in the past, you may want to put on a preventive application of fungicide such as maneb, captan or chlorothalnil.

Wilt Diseases

There are several soil-born organisms which attack the root system and plug up the vascular tissue causing wilting and eventual death of the tree. Especially susceptible are Silver Maple, Mimosa, and some oaks. Control is generally impossible; in some cases, a preventative soil sterilization program using Vapam in trenches between infected and healthy trees will restrict the spread of the disease. There are some Mimosa varieties which are resistant to fusarian wilt: Carlotte, Tryon, or US 64. These varieties are only resistant, however, and are not immune, so replanting in the same spot where you lost a tree from wilt, even with the resistant variety, will generally be unsuccessful.

Southern Fusiform Rust

Southern Fusiform Rust is particularly damaging to slash pine, one of the most commonly planted pines in the South. While there is some resistance to certain strains of the disease, unfortunately, little attention is paid to selection of a seed source from resistant trees for growing in a particular region. The disease appears as gall-like swellings which may completely surround a limb or trunk of a small tree. In early spring yellowish-orange blisters often appear from these swellings. The only control is to prune out infected limbs; if a tree trunk happens to be infected, there is little hope of recovery.

Live Oak Decline (*Cephalosporium* spp.)

Live oak decline may effect a number of trees in addition to live oaks. Sycamores are perhaps more susceptible to the disease organism than many oak species. Disease symptoms are exactly what you'd expect—a gradual dieback of the tree, with a characteristic resprouting along the main trunk and branches. Positive identification of the fungus is difficult; even if a tree is known to be infected with *Cephalosporium*, the organism can only be cultured out in the laboratory about one-third of the time. Even more unfortunate is the fact that no effective control measure has yet been devised. Benomyl will control the fungus, but it's difficult to get benomyl into the tree in a high enough concentration to save the tree. A number of special solvents have been utilized by Dr. E. P. Van Arsdel for this purpose, but at present many of these have been almost as damaging as the disease organism.

Southern Landscape Trees

(Because the deciduous trees have no foliage for up to four months of the year, the artist has illustrated their forms both bare and with foliage. The darker areas of the trees denote their winter forms; the shaded extremities represent their forms with full foliage.)

Small to Medium Deciduous Trees

Hercules-Club Prickly-Ash
Zanthoxylum clava-herculis

COMMON NAME: Hercules-Club Prickly-Ash
SCIENTIFIC NAME: *Zanthoxylum clava-herculis*
HEIGHT: 25'
SPREAD: 20'
ZONE: 8, Native as far north as Dallas
FORM: Small tree, with a broad, rounded crown

Culture. Prickly-Ash usually grows in sandy, well-drained soil but is quite tolerant and can be seen commonly along fence rows in the tight, clay soils of the Gulf Coast.

Suggested Uses. The Prickly-Ash has limited use in southern landscapes. It is of interest because of its medicinal uses. The leaves, inner bark, and prominent thorns of this tree are used as a home remedy for the relief of toothache. Chewing these portions of the plant will cause numbness and a tingling sensation.

Flowers. Insignificant; small, pale green.

Fruit. Although the fruit is not particularly ornamental, it is noticeable and is often eaten by birds. An Oriental species, *Zanthoxylum piperitum*, is the source of a condiment known as Japan Pepper used in the Orient.

Bark. The bark on this tree is quite noticeable from close range; it is marked with numerous stout thorns.

Foliage. The leaves of the Prickly Ash, besides providing toothache relief, are bright, shiny and fairly ornamental.

Remarks. The Prickly Ash is unavailable in the nursery trade but it is of some value as an ornamental plant. Where one is desired it will be necessary either to grow these trees from seed or collect them from the wild. They are commonly found growing along fences where they are protected from cultivation.

Eastern Redbud
Cercis canadensis

COMMON NAME: Eastern Redbud
SCIENTIFIC NAME: *Cercis canadensis*
HEIGHT: 30′
SPREAD: 15-25′
ZONE: 6; Hardy throughout the South
FORM: Small tree with a broad, rounded crown

Culture. Redbud trees prefer a loam soil, but they're rather tolerant and will eventually adapt to most soil conditions. Many people complain about difficulty in transplanting redbuds, but if care is taken not to set the plants lower than they originally grew, and if they are pruned back one-third to one-half their original size after transplanting, redbuds can be easily transplanted.

Suggested Uses. Redbud makes an ideal small flowering specimen tree which can be grown in fairly confined areas.

Flowers: Most redbuds produce pinkish-purple flowers; however, there are white-flowered forms and a number of improved pink-flowered forms.

Seed. Redbuds produce a large amount of seed that hangs on the tree much of the year. This is one of their main detracting features.

Bark. The bark is divided into narrow plates and is often gray to reddish-brown.

Foliage. The foliage of the redbud is one of its more attractive features. If not protected from insect and disease damage, it may make it look a bit ragged in the summer. Leaves are heart-shaped, and new spring growth often has a reddish tint. One variety, Forest Pansy, is grown specifically for its reddish-purple foliage, which is particularly noticeable in the spring.

Remarks. Redbuds are readily available; however, improved varieties are relatively unknown in the nursery trade. Other species worthy of trial in southern landscapes include: *Cercis occidentalis* (California Redbud), and *C. reniformis*, also referred to as *C. texensis* (Texas Redbud). Judas Tree (*C. siliquastrum*), a European species, is a common name sometimes used for our native redbud trees.

Redbud trees usually have a short to medium life span (25-50 years) and are susceptible to leaf-spotting fungi, borers, leaf feeding insects, root and wood rots. Spraying redbud trees in the spring, about the time the leaves are fully matured, and once or twice through the summer with a combination of an insecticide and fungicide may help to keep the tree looking neater during the summer and also result in a longer-lived tree. Borers can be controlled with sprays applied to the trunk utilizing lindane or BHC (see page 30).

Woolybucket Bumelia (Chittamwood)
Bumelia lanuginosa

COMMON NAME: Woolybucket Bumelia (Chittamwood)
SCIENTIFIC NAME: *Bumelia lanuginosa*
HEIGHT: 40′
SPREAD: 30′
ZONE: 6. This tree should be hardy in most of the South, but several other species, such as *B. schottii* (Spiniflora), *B. tenax*, and *B. celastrina* probably are not hardy much north of Houston.
FORM: Round-topped

Culture. The Chittamwood usually grows in sandy soils but is adapted to most soil types.

Suggested Uses. So many landscapes today need small- to medium-size shade trees; it's a shame bumelias have not been utilized more. This tree is an excellent plant for the small yard or as a townhouse shade tree.

Flowers. Bumelia has small white flowers clustered in the leaf axils. These flowers are an important source of honey in some areas.

Fruit. Bumelia produces small black fruits about ½ inch long.

Foliage. Most species are totally deciduous; however, a South Texas species, *B. schotti* (Spiniflora, also called *B. lanuginosa* v. *rigida*), is evergreen and probably hardy as far north as Houston.

Remarks. Bumelias are not readily available at nurseries, but they may be collected from the wild and can be relied upon for long life (50 years or more).

Huisache (Sweet Acacia)
Acacia farnesiana

COMMON NAME: Huisache (Sweet Acacia)
SCIENTIFIC NAME: *Acacia farnesiana*
HEIGHT: 30′
SPREAD: 15-20′
ZONE: 8
FORM: Open, spreading

Culture. Acacias are adapted to dry weather conditions, but Huisache does range eastward into east central Texas, along the Gulf Coast and into Florida. They are not easily transplanted and so aren't available. Small specimens growing in containers, however, can be handled easily. Existing trees should be saved if possible.

Suggested Uses: The Huisache makes an outstanding small flowering specimen tree which, because of its deep roots, makes for easy culture of grass or flowers underneath. It also has a rather open form and thus allows good sun penetration.

Flowers. Following a mild winter, especially in the upper range of this species, Acacias produce large numbers of small yellow fragrant flowers in ball-shaped clusters approximately ½ to ¾ inch in diameter. Flowers are intensely fragrant and, in fact, may be considered sickeningly sweet at close

range by some. The Dwarf Acacia *(Acacia tortuosa)* appears to have hardier bloom buds and will bloom almost every year in the Houston area.

Seed. Seed is produced in thickened, reddish-purple pods 2 to 3 inches long.

Bark. Reddish-brown.

Foliage. Foliage is fine-textured, deciduous.

Remarks. Huisache trees are generally unavailable in most nurseries except, perhaps, in small sizes (1- to 5-gallon cans). They are relatively long-lived trees, and although they do have prominent thorns up to an inch and a half long, they should be left in the landscape, particularly where they already exist. Huisache trees are victimized by twig girdlers which are very difficult to control because they're not feeding at the time they damage the tree. Instead, they're laying eggs. Picking up and destroying any small limbs which eventually break off due to twig girdler damage and spraying the trees with carbaryl in mid and late August will give some control.

Golden-Raintree
Koelreuteria formosana

COMMON NAME: Golden-Raintree
SCIENTIFIC NAME: *Koelreuteria formosana* (Chinese Flametree, *K. henryii, K. bipinnata*)
HEIGHT: 30′
SPREAD: 15-25′
ZONE: *K. formosana,* 9; *K. paniculata,* 5
FORM: Flat-topped, spreading

Culture. Golden-Raintrees are adapted to most soil types and are tolerant of most urban circumstances, including polluted air. Shallow roots and dense shade may make it difficult to grow grass under this tree.

Suggested Uses. Excellent flowering, medium-sized tree.

Flowers. The flowers of the Golden-Raintree are attractive, but they're not nearly as outstanding as the seed pods which follow. From a distance, they almost appear to be symptoms of iron chlorosis rather than flowers. There is considerable variation among seedlings in their ability to produce flowers and seed pods, so selection of superior grafted or budded varieties is direly needed. A Golden-Raintree that doesn't bloom may just be genetically inferior. Sun, however, is necessary for good bloom, and even superior trees may not bloom in the shade.

Fruit. This is the truly outstanding feature of the Gold-Raintree. *K. formosana* produces bright pinkish-red pods that look like small Chinese lanterns; the species *K. paniculata* produces less spectacular, brown seed pods. Seedlings may sometimes become a nuisance ·in flower beds.

Remarks. Golden-Raintrees are readily available but, again, the need for improved budded or grafted varieties cannot be overemphasized. One of the most frequent complaints about Golden-Raintrees is that they won't bloom. They are not long-lived trees—20 to 30 years is about average.

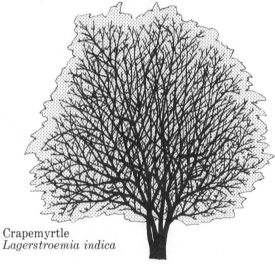

Crapemyrtle
Lagerstroemia indica

COMMON NAME: Crapemyrtle
SCIENTIFIC NAME: *Lagerstroemia indica*
HEIGHT: 35′
SPREAD: 15-25′
ZONE: 7
FORM: Small tree; often multiple trunk with a vased-shaped spread

Culture. Crapemyrtles require full sun to flower properly and to limit infection with powdery mildew. They are rather tolerant of soil types.

Suggested Uses. Crapemyrtles make outstanding small flowering specimen trees and can be grown in large containers of planter boxes. Particularly

adapted to this latter culture are some of the new dwarf varieties such as Petite Embers (rose-red), Petite Orchid (dark orchard), Petite Pinky (clear pink), Petite Red-Imp (dark red), Petite Ruby (deep ruby red), Petite Snow (white), Pink Ruffles (rosey pink), Royalty (rich, royal purple), Snow Baby (white), Tiny Fire (red), Firebird (watermelon red), Low Flame (red), and New Snow (white).

Flowers. Flowers are produced in large panicles in colors of white, pink, purple and watermelon red. A few varieties will repeat bloom; these include Potomac (medium pink), Seminole (medium pink), and Near East (flesh pink). D.R. Egolf of the National Arboretum is conducting breeding experiments with the objective of producing cultivars with mildew resistance, hardiness, true flower color, recurrent flowering, more desirable shrub and tree growth habits, and better autumn foliage coloration. Triploid hybrids which will repeat bloom without setting seed are a possibility in the future. The following list includes the best crapemyrtle cultivars in each color and height class*:

Dwarf (less than 3 feet)
Petite Embers—rose red
Petite Orchid—dark orchid
Petite Pinky—clear pink
Petite Red Imp—dark red
Petite Ruby—deep ruby red
Petite Snow—white
Pink Ruffles—rosy pink
Royalty—rich royal purple
Snow Baby—pure white
Tiny Fire—rich red

Semi-Dwarf (under 6 feet)
Dwarf Blue—lavender blue
Firebird—deep watermelon red, spreading growth
Low Flame—bright red
New Snow—white

Medium (6-12 feet)
Carolina Beauty—deep, bright red
Catawba—dark purple; dark foliage; highly mildew tolerant; brilliant orange-red autumn color
Cherokee—bright, clear red; truest red crapemyrtle
Conestoga—long tapered inflorescences, multicolored medium to light lavender, open growth
Imperial Pink—pastel pink
Near East—flesh pink, long flowering season, vigorous spreading

*Reprinted from *Horticulture*, August 1972, ©1972 by The Massachussetts Horticulture Society.

Pink Lace—clear, bright pink; similar to Near East

Powhatan—light lavender, mildew tolerant

Seminole—clear, medium pink, abundant, large inflorescences, recurrent bloom, mildew tolerant

Shell Pink—pale pink, similar to Near East

Twilight—dark purple, less hardy than most, upright

Tall (12 feet or more)

Country Red—dark red; similar to watermelon red

Dallas Red—dark red, upright

Dixie Brilliant—rich, deep watermelon red

Durant Red—pure red

Glendora White—large, showy with faint pink tint

Gray's Red—rich red, upright

Kellogg's Purple—rich purple, upright

Majestic Orchid—rich orchid, vigorous, upright

Potomac—medium pink, long flowering season with recurrent bloom, highly mildew tolerant, upright, vigorous

Red Star—deep watermelon red, long flower panicle, similar to William Toovey

William Toovey—dark watermelon red

Bark. Crapemyrtle bark is very thin and flakes off in irregular patches.

Foliage. Crapemyrtle foliage is deciduous, and some varieties, such as Catawba, have good, orange-red autumn color.

Remarks. The standard, or indica, crapemyrtle is readily available in most areas of the South, though named varieties usually are not. All too often the only identification that a crapemyrtle tree has in the nursery is a spot of paint, either white, pink, purple or red, to denote the flower color. That a number of outstanding varietal forms already exist, and that we can anticipate many more in the future, makes this oversimplification quite unfair. Crapemyrtles are long-lived trees, and old specimens attaining heights of 50-60 feet with a crown spread of 50 feet can be seen. Crapemyrtles do have insect and disease problems. Powdery mildew is particularly troublesome with most indica varieties. This disease can be

prevented by early spray applications of benomyl. They are also bothered by wax scale, an insect which sucks the juices out of the foliage and excretes a sticky material called honeydew on which a black, sooty mold eventually grows. This pest can be controlled by spraying diazinon or malathion once a week for three weeks.

Japanese Crapemyrtle
Lagerstroemia fauriei

COMMON NAME: Japanese Crapemyrtle
SCIENTIFIC NAME: *Lagerstroemia fauriei*
HEIGHT: 35′
SPREAD: 15 to 25′
ZONE: 8
FORM: Small; vase-shaped

Culture. Soil and culture requirements are about the same as for the indica crapemyrtle.

Suggested Uses. This crapemyrtle species is an outstanding specimen in itself. It has extreme vigor, disease resistance, and beautiful cinnamon-red bark. The Japanese Crapemyrtle makes a beautiful small- to medium-size flowering specimen tree.

Flowers. The flowers are white and are produced in much smaller panicles than most of the indica varieties, but this crapemyrtle flowers profusely and makes an attractive landscape tree.

Bark. The bark of the Japanese Crapemyrtle is one of the tree's outstanding features. When it peels off (about the time the tree blooms), it is a beautiful cinnamon red, contrasting with light brown.

Foliage. The foliage of the Japanese crapemyrtle is more pointed than most indica varieties and, unfortunately, does not produce any fall color.

Remarks. One of the chief assets of this tree is its resistance to powdery mildew, a serious disease of most indica varieties. The tree is not readily available, but as it becomes more well known it should be easier to find because it is relatively easy to propagate from vigorous hardwood or semi-hardwood cuttings. The trees are apparently long-lived.

The Japanese Crapemyrtle is susceptible to the same scale insects that plague indica varieties.

mildew resistance characteristic of the fauriei parent.

They are susceptible to scale, as are the other crapemyrtles, but they have great potential for future landscape use in the South.

Jerusalem Thorn
Parkinsonia aculeata

COMMON NAME: Jerusalem Thorn
SCIENTIFIC NAME: *Parkinsonia aculeata*
HEIGHT: 35′
SPREAD: 15 to 25′
ZONE: 8
FORM: Open tree; often asymmetrical

Culture. Parkinsonia is well adapted to a variety of soils; it is popular because it grows in well-drained, dry areas.

Suggested Uses. The Jerusalem Thorn fits in very well with the southwestern style of architecture. It allows ample sunlight to filter through, and its deep root system permits growing other plants such as daylilies or annual flowers on the ground beneath.

Flowers. Yellow flowers are produced over a long period of time during late spring and summer.

Foliage. The foliage of Jerusalem Thorn is very fine-textured and not the least bit messy, making this tree particularly useful near swimming pools or any place where debris would be a problem.

Remarks. Jerusalem Thorn is relatively available in many southern nurseries, at least in seedling form. No doubt, improved varieties could be selected and propagated by cuttings, grafting or budding. It is not an extremely long-lived tree—25 to 35 years is normal. It is tolerant of salt drift and soil salinity, so it can be used near the seashore.

Scale insects may cause some problems.

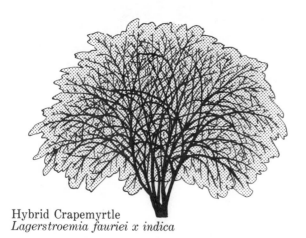

Hybrid Crapemyrtle
Lagerstroemia fauriei x indica

COMMON NAME: Hybrid Crapemyrtle
SCIENTIFIC NAME: *Lagerstroemia fauriei x indica*
HEIGHT: 35′
SPREAD: 25 to 35′
ZONE: 7
FORM: Small; vase-shaped

Culture. Same as for indica crapemyrtle.

Suggested Uses. Specimen flowering tree.

Flowers. So far, the flower color in these hybrids has been limited to white and purple in selections produced at the National Arboretum and pinkish-lavender hybrid found by Mr. Bill Basham in Houston, Texas.

Bark. This crapemyrtle, too, has attractive bark. Some have the cinnamon-red bark characteristic of the fauriei parent; others have varying shades of red to dark brown bark which contrasts with the lighter buff-colored bark remaining on the tree.

Foliage. From selections being produced at the National Arboretum, it seems that hybrid varieties with fall foliage color are a likelihood in the near future.

Remarks. This tree has almost unbelievable vigor, and most of the hybrid varieties have retained the

Mesquite
Prosopis glandulosa (*P. juliflora*)

COMMON NAME: Mesquite
SCIENTIFIC NAME: *Prosopis glandulosa*
(*P. juliflora*)
HEIGHT: 20 to 50'
SPREAD: 20 to 40'
ZONE: 8
FORM: Wide, spreading tree which often gives the impression of a shiny-leaved weeping willow when well cared for.

Culture. Mesquite trees are relatively tolerant of soils, although they naturally occur in sandy, dry locations.

Suggested Uses. Where mesquite trees exist they can be left as medium-size shade trees.

Flowers. Flowers are greenish-white, fragrant but not particularly noticeable.

Seed Pods. Narrow pods 5 to 8 inches long are produced on common species, but another species, Screw-pod mesquite (*P. pubescens*), produces very distinctive spiral pods 1 to 2 inches long.

Foliage. The foliage of mesquite trees is fine-textured and allows plenty of light penetration.

Remarks. Because it is deep-rooted and will respond to a little water and fertilizer, mesquite trees should get more consideration for southern landscapes. There are a number of species, and the nomenclature for identifying them is somewhat confusing. The "typical" species is the Honey mesquite (*P. glandulosa*). Other species include Velvet mesquite (*P. glandulosa velutina*), Torry mesquite (*P. glandulosa torreyna*), and dwarf mesquite (*P. reptans*). None of these species are readily available in nurseries, and, because they have a large tap root, they're probably difficult to transplant from the wild except in small sizes. Mesquite is rather long-lived and makes a nice medium-size shade tree when properly cared for.

Red Buckeye
Aesculus pavia

COMMON NAME: Red Buckeye
SCIENTIFIC NAME: *Aesculus pavia*
HEIGHT: 20'
SPREAD: 10 to 15'
ZONE: 5
FORM: Small, oval-shaped specimen tree

Culture. Best planted as an understory tree or mulched to reduce competition from the lawn. Appreciates moist, fertile soil.

Suggested Uses. Red Buckeye is a good small tree for use in landscapes where space is minimal.

Flowers. Red to reddish-purple spikes of small, showy flowers.

Seed. 1½ to 2-inch round capsule.

Foliage. Large compound leaves; yellow fall color.

Remarks. This tree is relatively unavailable but should be grown more.

Sumac
Rhus copallina (Flame-leafed sumac)

COMMON NAME: Sumac
SCIENTIFIC NAME: *Rhus copallina* (Flame-leaf sumac), *R. glabra* (Smooth sumac, *R. lanceolata* (Prairie sumac)

HEIGHT: 10 to 20'
SPREAD: 5 to 10'
ZONE: 2
FORM: Small tree, large shrub

Culture. Sumacs are usually found growing in a sandy loam soil, but they are fairly adaptable to soil conditions.

Suggested Uses. Sumacs make outstanding small specimen trees which should be used more for small home or townhouse lots.

Flowers. Large clusters of white flowers are produced in the spring.

Fruit. Large clusters of brown to red seed heads.

Foliage. Brilliant red fall color is one of the outstanding attributes of the sumacs.

Remarks. Sumac trees are not readily available, but they may be collected in the wild.

Flowers. Almost all the hawthorns adapted to the South have white flowers, though a pink form of Parsley Hawthorn is sometimes found.

Fruit. Most species produce a red fruit; the Blueberry Hawthorn (*C. brachyacantha*) has, as expected, blue berries.

Bark. The bark on many species of hawthorns, including Parsley Hawthorn, peels and flakes off in an attractive manner. Many species have short spines.

Foliage. The foliage on Parsley Hawthorn is especially attractive; it has the fine texture and appearance of parsley leaves and the bright glossy look typical of many hawthorns.

Remarks. Hawthorns are quite susceptible to aphids, or plant lice, which attack new growth early in the spring. Scale insects attack the trees later during the year. One species, the Mayhaw (*C. opaqua*), is particularly interesting because it produces a rather large fruit (as large as ¾ inch across) which makes a delicious jelly. This latter species is adapted to swampy soils.

Parsley Hawthorn
Crataegus marshalli

COMMON NAME: Parsley Hawthorn
SCIENTIFIC NAME: *Crataegus marshalli*
HEIGHT: 20'
SPREAD: 10 to 15'
ZONE: 6
FORM: Small, rounded, flowering tree

Culture. Appreciates a loose, well-draining soil or a clay soil which has been improved with several inches of organic matter such as pine bark or peat moss. Will grow in partial shade but blooms and fruits best in full sun.

Suggested Uses. The hawthorns, and the Parsley Hawthorn in particular, make outstanding, small flowering specimen trees in the landscape.

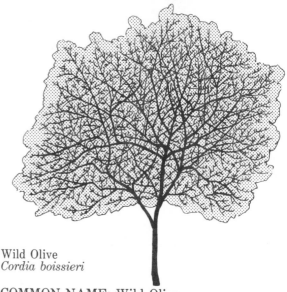

Wild Olive
Cordia boissieri

COMMON NAME: Wild Olive
SCIENTIFIC NAME: *Cordia boissieri*
HEIGHT: 20'
SPREAD: 10 to 15'
ZONE: 9
FORM: Small, irregular-shaped flowering tree

Culture. Rather tolerant of soil types but particularly adapted to sandy, dry soils and full sun.

Suggested Uses. The Wild Olive makes an excellent small flowering, specimen tree which blooms over a long period of time.

Flowers. White petunia-like flowers are produced in spring through early summer.

Fruit. A greenish olive-looking fruit which, though edible, should not be consumed in large quantities.

Foliage. Leaves have a velvety texture and are light green to grayish in color.

Remarks. Wild Olive is not reliably hardy much north of Houston and actually is best located in a protected area even along the Gulf Coast. Another species of Cordia, the Geiger tree (*C. sebestena*), produces red flowers and is commonly grown in tropical regions of Florida. Perhaps by combining these two species we could obtain a hardier form with a different range of flower color.

Berlandier's acacia (Guajillo)
Acacia berlandieri

COMMON NAME: Berlandier's acacia (Guajillo)
SCIENTIFIC NAME: *Acacia berlandieri*
HEIGHT: 15′
SPREAD: 10 to 15′
ZONE: 8
FORM: Low-branching, short-trunked, rounded growth habit

Culture. Although this plant comes from Central and West Texas, where the climate is arid, it will grow well considerably east of its native range if good drainage and full sun are provided.

Suggested Uses. Berlandier's acacia works well as a small specimen tree or for a background planting in place of large shrubs. It can also be grown in large containers.

Flowers. Guajillo is one of the most famous honey plants of Texas. Flowers are typically acacia-like and white in color.

Foliage. Foliage is deciduous and very fine-textured, making this tree very useful where low maintenance is desired.

Remarks. Guajillo is not readily available in nurseries, though it can be found in some. Small plants can be collected from the wild, and the trees are easily grown from seed.

Fringe Tree
Chionanthus virginicus

COMMON NAME: Fringe Tree
SCIENTIFIC NAME: *Chionanthus virginicus*
HEIGHT: 15 to 25′
SPREAD: 10 to 20′
ZONE: 4
FORM: Small, flowering tree or large shrub, narrow oblong crown

Culture. The Fringe Tree, or Old Man's Beard as it's sometimes called, is one of the many understory trees found in the forest. It likes a loose, acid soil and grows quite well in partial shade.

Suggested Uses. In nature, the Fringe Tree grows best along the edge of the forest and thus makes a good background tree, although it may occasionally be used as a specimen plant.

Flowers. The flowers are produced in loose, drooping panicles. Individual flowers have slender ¾-inch petals.

Remarks. Fringe Trees are not readily available, although they can be found in some specialty nurseries and can be ordered in small sizes from mail order sources. An oriental species, *C. ratusus*, may also be available from specialty nurseries. Fringe Trees are late bringing out foliage in the spring, giving the appearance of being dead. Scale insects are sometimes a problem.

Edible Pear
Pyrus communis

COMMON NAME: Edible Pear
SCIENTIFIC NAME: *Pyrus communis*
HEIGHT: 50′
SPREAD: 25 to 30′
ZONE: 5
FORM: Upright

Culture. Most soils will do. Pears are best when grown with minimum of fertilization, watering or anything else that would tend to stimulate excessive vegetative growth, which is succulent and very susceptible to fire blight. However, an occasional fungicide spray to prevent leaf spotting and defoliation is important, since the tree will attempt to replace lost foliage in late summer, thus robbing itself of food reserves which would be used for the production of pears.

Suggested Uses. The Edible Pear varieties can be used in place of other flowering trees, though their growth habit is often asymmetrical, and, unless the fruit is consumed, it will be a litter problem.

Flowers. Edible Pears, like the ornamental varieties, also produce beautiful white flowers.

Fruit. Fruit forms vary considerably, but most southern varieties are hybrids between the Sand Pear (*P. pyrifolia*) and the European varieties (*P. communis*). The fruit of many varities, such as Kieffer and Garber, is extremely hard and thus difficult to consume when fresh; therefore, it is usually used in the preparation of canned fruit, jellies or jams. Some better-quality varieties are: Orient, Ayres, Pineapple, Baldwin, and Maxine.

Remarks. Many pear varieties are available, but just because a variety is offered for sale doesn't mean it's adapted to your region. All too often varieties like Bartlett and Anjou are sold in the deep South but are not adapted.

In addition to leaf-spotting fungus which may defoliate pear trees, fire blight, bacterial disease, may seriously damage blooms, twigs, leaves and older areas of the bark. During mild wet periods in the spring, cankers (sores) caused by the bacterium begin to ooze bacterial cells which are then splashed by rain and carried by bees to the flowers where infection occurs and eventually progresses into the twigs, at which point the limbs may appear burned or blackened, and hence the name "fire blight." Spraying with a copper fungicide or an antibotic during the blooming period is important if fire blight is to be controlled chemically, but even more important is the selection of resistant varieties such as Orient, Kieffer and Baldwin.

Callery Pear
Pyrus calleryana

COMMON NAME: Callery Pear
SCIENTIFIC NAME: *Pyrus calleryana*
HEIGHT: 30′
SPREAD: 10-20′
ZONE: 4
FORM: Small flowering tree

Culture. Same as for Edible Pear.

Suggested Uses. Small flowering specimen tree.

Flowers. Abundant white flowers produced in the early spring.

Fruit. Fruit is small and insignificant.

Foliage. Deciduous.

Remarks. There are a number of low-chilling seedling varieties of Callery Pear which could be selected and utilized more efficiently in the deep South. A variety called 'Bradford' has done extremely well in some areas of the mid-South and further north, but in the Houston area it rarely, if ever, blooms. Callery Pear is somewhat resistant to fire blight, but not totally, and there is much variation in this resistance among seedlings. Other varieties include: 'Aristocrat,' 'Chanticleer' (pyramidal form), 'Fauriei' (dwarf), and 'Rancho.' The value of these cultivars in the deep South has not been determined.

Tulip Magnolia
Magnolia soulangeana

COMMON NAME: Tulip Magnolia
SCIENTIFIC NAME: *Magnolia soulangeana*
HEIGHT: 25′
SPREAD: 10 to 15′
ZONE: 5
FORM: Deciduous, small flowering tree

Culture. Appreciates a sandy, acid soil but will grow in a well-prepared clay soil.

Suggested Uses. Makes a very striking landscape specimen.

Flowers. Flowers vary from white to dark purple, depending on the variety, and are very beautiful if not frozen during budding, which often happens in many areas of the South.

Foliage. The leaves on most of the deciduous magnolias are not as bright and glossy as they are on the evergreen magnolias like Southern Magnolia.

Remarks. Tulip Trees or Tulip Magnolias are readily available in nurseries, but there are many different hybrid varieties that need to be evaluated more for use in the South.

Jujube
Zizyphus jujuba

COMMON NAME: Jujube
SCIENTIFIC NAME: *Zizyphus jujuba*
HEIGHT: 30′
SPREAD: 10-20′
ZONE: 7
FORM: Open, may form thickets

Culture. Grows almost anywhere and will withstand dry soil, heat, and alkaline soils.

Suggested Uses. As background planting, large screen.

Flowers. Insignificant.

Fruit. Approximately an inch long, edible. Color varies from dark red to black.

Foliage. Deciduous.

Remarks. Due to its messy fruit, the jujube is not a low-maintenance tree but it may be of value where it can be appreciated and utilized for its date-like fruit.

Texas Sophora
Sophora affinis

COMMON NAME: Texas Sophora
SCIENTIFIC NAME: *Sophora affinis*

HEIGHT: 20'
SPREAD: 10 to 15'
ZONE: 6
FORM: Medium-size shade tree

Culture: Easily grown in almost any soil. Flower production will be greatest in full sun.

Suggested Uses. Texas Sophora is not an especially showy plant, but it does have noticeable flowers and very interesting seed pods. It is a practical size for today's smaller landscapes.

Flowers. Sweetpea-like, white and pink.

Seed Pods. Black bean pods with a narrow constriction between each of the seeds; hence the nickname "necklace tree."

Bark. The bark on the trunk is gray; the small branches are light green.

Remarks. There are a number of *Sophoras* cultivated as ornamentals. This would make an interesting inclusion in a breeding program.

Persimmon
Diospyros virginiana

COMMON NAME: Persimmon
SCIENTIFIC NAME: *Diospyros virginiana*
HEIGHT: 50'
SPREAD: 20-30'
ZONE: 4
FORM: Oval-crowned small tree, may form thickets

Culture. Full sun. Tolerant of most soils, will respond to fertilization, insect and disease control.

Suggested Uses. Persimmon trees come in both male and female forms. Because the females produce messy fruit, the male form is more desirable for landscape uses. They make good small- to medium-size shade trees.

Flowers. Inconspicuous but rather fragrant flowers.

Fruit. The fruit is small, 1½ inches in diameter, and varies in color from yellow to orange. A common misconception is that the fruit is not edible until after a frost. Some varieties have very little astringency.

Bark. The bark of a mature persimmon tree is interestingly divided into rectangular chunks.

Foliage. The deciduous foliage colors well in autumn, varying from yellow to a deep purple.

Remarks. Persimmon trees are not readily available in nurseries. Some specialty nurseries may offer them, and there is quite a bit of potential for selection of large-fruited varieties from those trees that already exist in the wild. Larger persimmons are difficult to transplant. Webworms often attack foliage.

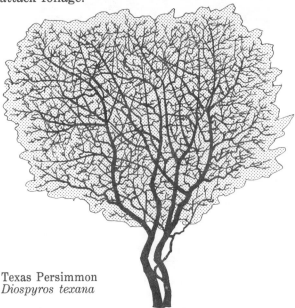

Texas Persimmon
Diospyros texana

COMMON NAME: Texas Persimmon
SCIENTIFIC NAME: *Diospyros texana*
HEIGHT: 30'
SPREAD: 10-15'
ZONE: 8
FORM: Small deciduous tree, slow to drop its leaves, though.

Culture. Tolerant of alkaline soils.

Suggested Uses. Small specimen tree.

Flowers. Insignificant but rather fragrant.

Fruit. Black, one inch in diameter.

Bark. Smooth, almost white to gray, very ornamental.

Foliage. Fine to medium texture, late in falling.

Remarks. Since there are both male and female trees of this species, the male trees are preferred because of the messy fruit of the females.

late (produce primarily female flowers). In some years certain varieties may produce pistillate, stamenate (male) and perfect flowers all at the same time; in other years they may produce primarily female or male flowers. Fruit maturity is most likely to occur if male flowers of compatible varieties are produced and seed is set in the fruit.

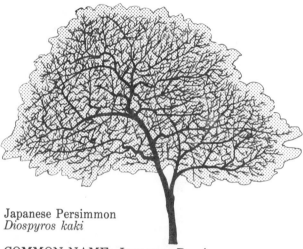

Japanese Persimmon
Diospyros kaki

COMMON NAME: Japanese Persimmon
SCIENTIFIC NAME: *Diospyros kaki*
HEIGHT: 40′
SPREAD: 20-30′
ZONE: 7
FORM: Small, fruiting tree

Culture. Of easy culture, full sun required for good fruit production. Trees subjected to stress due to insufficient water, too much water, insect damage, etc., may drop fruit.

Suggested Uses. This is a very ornamental and productive small fruiting tree.

Flowers. Insignificant.

Fruit. A number of varieties are available, including 'Fuyu,' 'Hachiya,' 'Tane-na-shi' and 'Tamopan.' Most do not produce seed. Because of this lack of seed there is a low hormone content in the fruit, which is why it often drops during stress.

Foliage. Deciduous. May be red-orange in the fall.

Remarks. The most readily available variety of Japanese Persimmon is 'Tane-na-shi.' Since most varieties are grafted onto common persimmon root stock, they are often dwarfed in comparison to the size that they may attain in the Orient. Scale insects may be a problem. Most varieties are pistil-

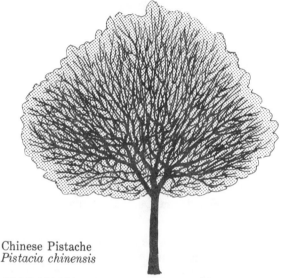

Chinese Pistache
Pistacia chinensis

COMMON NAME: Chinese Pistache
SCIENTIFIC NAME: *Pistacia chinensis*
HEIGHT: 50′
SPREAD: 25-35′
ZONE: 6
FORM: Small- to medium-size round-topped shade tree

Culture. Full sun. Tolerant of urban conditions, appreciates a well-drained soil. It is deep-rooted and drought-tolerant.

Suggested Uses. This is an ideal size tree for small landscapes.

Flowers. Insignificant.

Fruit. Small, red, forming dense clusters; this tree is sexual, and only the females produce fruit.

Foliage. Deciduous; some varieties provide good fall color, varying from yellow to brilliant red and orange, even in the lower South.

Remarks. The Chinese Pistache is a very useful tree, but it is necessary to male specimens which have good form and fall color. It is relatively free of insects and diseases and should be rather long-lived.

American Hornbean
Carpinus carolinina

COMMON NAME: American Hornbean
SCIENTIFIC NAME: *Carpinus carolinina*
HEIGHT: 35'
SPREAD: 15-20'
ZONE: 3
FORM: Small crooked tree

Culture. Needs adequate soil moisture in sun or partial shade.

Suggested Uses. This tree is not readily available in nurseries and it is difficult to transplant except when small. In landscapes where it already exists, the American Hornbean is worth saving.

Flowers. Insignificant.

Seed. Small nutlet attached to a three-lobed leaf-like structure.

Foliage. Deciduous, smooth yellow in fall.

Remarks. Slow-growing, interesting smooth bark. Could be used more.

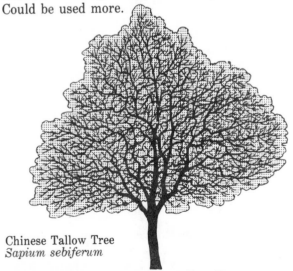

Chinese Tallow Tree
Sapium sebiferum

COMMON NAME: Chinese Tallow Tree
SCIENTIFIC NAME: *Sapium sebiferum*

HEIGHT: 40'
SPREAD: 15-25'
ZONE: 9
FORM: Small, round-topped shade tree

Culture. Full sun.

Suggested Uses. Small specimen or shade tree.

Flowers. The flowers, though not particularly showy, are an excellent source of honey.

Seed. White seed is produced in the fall, but it often turns black with mildew before its attractiveness can be appreciated.

Foliage. The Chinese Tallow is one of the most reliable fall coloring trees in the lower South. Color varies from yellow to orange to deep purple.

Remarks. So many tallow trees are planted in the South that surely several superior varieties could be budded or grafted. The tree forms shallow roots which are very vigorous and competitive, but this is otherwise a relatively long-lived tree with few problems.

Western Soapberry
Sapindus drummondii

COMMON NAME: Western Soapberry
SCIENTIFIC NAME: *Sapindus drummondii*
HEIGHT: 50'
SPREAD: 25-35'
ZONE: 5
FORM: Small oval shade tree

Culture. Tolerant of most soils, easily grown in full sun.

Suggested Uses. An attractive small shade tree.

Flowers. Large white clusters.

Fruit. Round, yellowish translucent fruit, with one seed. Hangs on the trees through much of the winter. The fruit is fairly attractive although it may become a nuisance if youngsters discover that it works better than spit balls. The fruit can also be used in place of soap.

Bark. The bark peals off and is relatively attractive.

Foliage. Deciduous; good yellow fall color.

Remarks. The Western Soapberry is not readily available. It's a very tough, drought-tolerant tree, subject to few pests, and could be used much more in southern landscapes with some selection for improved varieties. Scale insects may occasionally damage the tree.

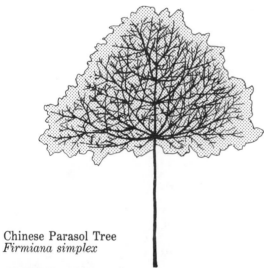

Chinese Parasol Tree
Firmiana simplex

COMMON NAME: Chinese Parasol Tree
SCIENTIFIC NAME: *Firmiana simplex*
HEIGHT: 40'
SPREAD: 10-15'
ZONE: 8
FORM: Tall, upright, tropical-looking tree

Culture. Fast-growing, tolerant of most soils.

Suggested Uses. This tree has such a unique form and appearance that its use is somewhat difficult in most landscapes.

Flowers. Insignificant.

Bark. The bark on this tree is a prominent bright green, unlike the common brown scales or plates seen on most trees.

Foliage. Deciduous; similar in shape to sycamore leaves, but brighter green and very large.

Remarks. This is an extremely fast-growing tree, and, as with most fast-growing trees, it is rather short-lived.

Serviceberry
Amelanchier arborea

COMMON NAME: Serviceberry
SCIENTIFIC NAME: *Amelanchier arborea*
HEIGHT: 25'
SPREAD: 10-15'
ZONE: 6
FORM: Small flowering understory tree

Culture. Serviceberry trees require the same conditions as dogwood trees—sandy soil and partial shade. In some parts of the world they are cultivated extensively for their edible fruit. Russia is reportedly growing Serviceberry as a commercial crop.

Suggested Uses. Serviceberry can be used as a nice small flowering tree. Fruit production, without further breeding to improve size and quality, is insignificant, but this species does have potential as a source of food for wildlife, and development of large-fruited forms is possible.

Flowers. Large racemes of white flowers are produced in the early spring and are followed by reddish-purple berries. The flowers are very ornamental but may fall from the tree quickly. The fruit is soon consumed by birds after ripening.

Foliage. Deciduous.

Remarks. Amelanchiers have not been cultivated to any great extent in the South, but they do have potential. Since they're members of the rose family, they are susceptible to fire blight and several insect pests.

American Hop-Hornbean
Ostrya virginiana

COMMON NAME: American Hop-Hornbean
SCIENTIFIC NAME: *Ostrya virginiana*
HEIGHT: 50'
SPREAD: 20-30'
ZONE: 3
FORM: Small- to medium-size shade tree

Culture. Usually found in sandy, acid soils on upland sites. Tolerant of a wide range of conditions.

Flowers. Insignificant.

Seed. Produced in cone-like clusters.

Foliage. Deciduous; rough.

Remarks. This tree is not available in nurseries but where it exists in the native landscape it should be spared. It is difficult to transplant from the woods but could be grown more successfully as a nursery plant.

Mexican Plum
Prunus mexicana

COMMON NAME: Mexican Plum
SCIENTIFIC NAME: *Prunus mexicana*
HEIGHT: 25'

SPREAD: 10-15'
ZONE: 6
FORM: Small flowering tree

Culture. Widely adapted to a variety of soils, needs full sun for best flower and fruit production but will grow in partial shade.

Suggested Uses. One of the most delightful small flowering trees for southern landscapes.

Flowers. Small, white, extremely fragrant flowers. One tree per block will perfume the whole neighborhood.

Fruit. Small, approximately 1½ inches in diameter, dark purplish-red with a white waxy bloom.

Bark. Peels off, or exfoliates, easily.

Foliage. Deciduous, rough-textured.

Remarks. This tree is not readily available in nurseries but is easily grown and transplanted, so it is a good subject for nursery production. As with all fruit trees, if not sprayed, even this wild variety will have worms in the fruit. The fruit is quite variable but generally makes an excellent jelly.

Texas Red Oak (Spanish Oak)
Quercus texana

COMMON NAME: Texas Red Oak (Spanish Oak)
SCIENTIFIC NAME: *Quercus texana*
HEIGHT: 35-50'
SPREAD: 25-35'
ZONE: 5
FORM: Medium-size shade tree, pyramidal or round-topped

Culture. Adapts to various soils, including alkaline soils, where iron chlorosis might be a problem with other species of red oak.

Suggested Uses. Texas Red Oak makes an outstanding medium- to large-size shade tree.

Foliage. Red fall color is often evident even in southern ranges.

Remarks. Texas Oak is becoming readily available in Texas, especially in San Antonio and Dallas. Closely related species such as Shumard Oak (*Q. shumardi*) and Nuttall Oak (*Q. nuttallii*) are perhaps better adapted to eastern regions of the South. These last two species often attain a height of 100 feet or more.

Southern Crabapple
Malus angustifolia

COMMON NAME: Southern Crabapple
SCIENTIFIC NAME: *Malus angustifolia*
HEIGHT: 35′
SPREAD: 15-25′
ZONE: 6
FORM: Small, rounded, flowering tree

Culture. This tree is easily grown. Though it will grow in partial shade, it needs sun to bloom and fruit properly.

Suggested Uses. Good as a small flowering tree in the landscape.

Flowers. The flowers of the Southern Crabapple species that grow in the deep South and that are adapted to areas along the Gulf Coast are not as spectacular as those of varieties adapted to more northern regions, where greater tolerance of winter chilling is obtained, resulting in favorable growth. One variety, 'Eley,' is satisfactory as far south as College Station, Texas. There is great potential for development of low-chilling crabapple varieties which would add much to our southern landscapes.

Fruit. Approximately one inch in diameter, usually pale yellowish-green and often fragrant, the fruit of the Southern Crabapple is suitable for use in making jelly or perserves, but its small size makes this a tedious chore.

Foliage. Deciduous.

Remarks. Some insects and diseases can be a problem, chiefly scale and cedar-apple rust. However, due to the relatively limited number of these trees, especially in the deep South along the Gulf Coast, pest problems should be minimal.

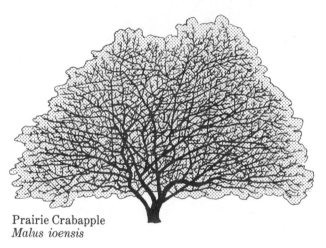

Prairie Crabapple
Malus ioensis

COMMON NAME: Prairie Crabapple
SCIENTIFIC NAME: *Malus ioensis*
HEIGHT: 10-25′
SPREAD: 10-20′
ZONE: 5
FORM: Small, rounded, flowering tree

Culture. Readily adapts to most soils. The Texas Crabapple, or Blanco Crabapple, is adapted to dry western areas of the South as well as to the Southeast.

Suggested Uses. This tree, just like the Southern Crabapple, could stand a great deal of selection and improvement as well as crossing with more ornamental varieties adapted to northern areas.

Flowers. White or pink, fragrant in clusters of two to five.

Fruit. Greenish-yellow, approximately 1½ inch in diameter. The Texas Crabapple (Blanco Crabapple) has very aromatic fruit.

Foliage. Deciduous.

Remarks. Species adapted to the lower South are generally in short supply, and some of the subspecies listed may be rather rare.

Sassafras
Sassafras albidum

COMMON NAME: Sassafras
SCIENTIFIC NAME: *Sassafras albidum*
HEIGHT: 50'
SPREAD: 20-30'
ZONE: 4
FORM: Variable, upright to flattened, oblong depending on whether it is grown under forest conditions or in the open, often forming thickets.

Culture. Where well adapted this tree may become a pest, but it does need sandy, acid soil, and it is difficult to transplant in large sizes.

Flowers. Rather noticeable, yellowish-green, though the individual flowers are not spectacular.

Fruit. Male and female plants exist and, of course, only females produce fruit. Ripened fruit is rarely seen on a Sassafras tree because it is a favorite of many bird species.

Foliage. Beautiful fall color is one of the principal merits of the Sassafras tree; it is also of interest because at least three leaf forms are found on the tree at one time—regular lanceloate leaves as well as two- and three-fingered mitten-shaped leaves. The foliage is used in the preparation of gumbo filé and the roots are used for sassfras tea.

Remarks. In tight, clay soils or in soils where the pH is neutral-to-alkaline, considerable soil preparation is necessary. Incorporating 2 to 3 inches of organic matter along with 1 to 2 pounds

of sulfur per 100 square feet to make the soil well-drained and acid will make Sassafras trees happy. They are best transplanted in small sizes and should be used much more in southern landscapes.

Two-winged Silverbell
Halesia diptera

COMMON NAME: Two-winged Silverbell
SCIENTIFIC NAME: *Halesia diptera*
HEIGHT: 30'
SPREAD: 15-20'
ZONE: 7
FORM: Small flowering tree

Culture. Silverbell is often found growing under the same conditions as Dogwood: sandy, acid soil and partial shade. It seems to be less demanding of these circumstances than Dogwood, howevever.

Flowers. White, bell-like, hung along the small branches.

Seed Pod. Seed is enclosed in a pod with two broad wings.

Foliage. Soft, light green, deciduous leaves.

Remarks. Unfortunately, this small understory tree is often one of the first to be cleared during development of subdivisions in wooded areas, and it is not common in cultivation. Several other species of *Halesia* are available, including *H. carolina*, a more northern variety, and *H. parviflora*. Neither of these latter species has as much potential for use in the South as does *H. diptera*.

Southern Blackhaw Viburnum
Viburnum rufidulum

COMMON NAME: Southern Blackhaw Viburnum
SCIENTIFIC NAME: *Viburnum rufidulum*
HEIGHT: 15-25'
SPREAD: 10-20'
ZONE: 5

FORM: Small flowering tree

Culture. Easily grown in most soils, but appreciates a well-prepared loose soil. Addition of several inches of organic matter such as pine bark, peat moss, rice hulls or compost to the top 6 to 8 inches of soil, or planting in a raised bed if tight wet soils are a problem, will be beneficial.

Flowers. White, showy but rather susceptible to weather damage; short-lasting.

Fruit. Bluish-black berries in late summer and fall.

Foliage. Deciduous, but may be slow to defoliate in southern areas. Some varieties have brilliant red fall color.

Remarks. This tree is worthy of greater propagation because it produces flowers in spring, has brilliant color in the fall, and is a small tree suited to smaller landscapes.

Large Deciduous Trees

Riverbirch
Betula nigra

COMMON NAME: Riverbirch

SCIENTIFIC NAME: *Betula nigra*
HEIGHT: 90'
SPREAD: 20-30'
ZONE: 4
FORM: Often multi-trunked, slender-crowned tree

Culture. Tolerant of wet soils. If subjected to drought stress, it may defoliate with subsequent dieback of small twigs.

Suggested Uses. Very attractive specimen tree.

Bark. The bark on this tree has outstanding ornamental features—contrasting reddish-brown and white peeling, curling flakes.

Foliage. Delicate, sparse leaves.

Remarks. It's important to select large-size specimens of Riverbirch since not all have the outstanding bark characteristics which make this tree a valuable ornamental.

Sugar Maple
Acer saccharum

COMMON NAME: Sugar Maple
SCIENTIFIC NAME: *Acer saccharum*
HEIGHT: 75'
SPREAD: 50-60'
ZONE: 3
FORM: Large shade tree, oval to rounded crown

Culture. Sugar Maples are usually grown in rich, well-drained soils, but Mr. Lynn Lowery, nurseryman in the Houston area, reports that Sugar Maples from a southern seed source have been transplanted and are growing well in the tight, clay soils of the Gulf Coast.

Flowers. Insignificant.

Seed. Small winged samaras, usually brown.

Foliage. Deciduous.

Remarks. The Sugar Maples grown from southern seed sources have considerable potential in the South, but their propagation has been extremely limited. A similar species, the Florida Sugar Maple (*A. barbatum*, height 40-60'), also grows naturally in the South. The latter species may very well be a variety of Sugar Maple, although it has smaller leaves. Another maple species, *A. grandidentatum sinuosum* (height 30-50'), is particularly adapted to the South and is tolerant of alkaline soils, which is not surprising since it is native to central Texas. It turns a brilliant red orange in the fall, and has potential for many areas of the South,

but especially the Southwest. A similar cultivar is *A. saccharum* 'Caddo' from southwestern Oklahoma. The Box-Elder Maple (*A. negundo*, height 30-50') is adapted to the South but is rather short-lived, weak-wooded and generally undesirable. Trident Maple (*A. buergerianum*, height 20-40 feet), a species introduced from Japan, is well adapted to the South and deserves wider use.

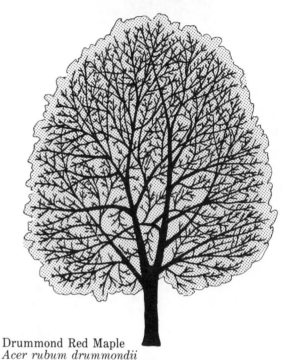

Drummond Red Maple
Acer rubum drummondii

COMMON NAME: Drummond Red Maple
SCIENTIFIC NAME: *Acer rubrum drummondii*
HEIGHT: 120'
SPREAD: 40-50'
ZONE: 6
FORM: Fast-growing, narrow-crowned shade tree.

Culture. Easily grown, best adapted to sandy, acid soils.

Flowers. Beautiful red clusters of flowers are very showy in late winter or early spring (January in the Houston, Texas area).

Fruit. Interesting seed produced in red samaras which flutter to the ground.

Foliage. In the fall the foliage of better varieties is a brilliant red, sometimes mixed with yellow.

Remarks. Southern species of red maple, such as the Drummond Red Maple, are relatively good, fast-growing trees. Though somewhat short-lived (50 years) and weak-wooded, they still make good landscape trees. Although the Silver Maple (*A. sac-*

charinum) is often sold in the deep South, it is not well adapted and at best makes a medium-size tree. It is very susceptible to wax scale and has very weak wood. Its main attribute seems to be that it transplants easily.

Sweetgum
Liquidambar styraciflua

COMMON NAME: Sweetgum
SCIENTIFIC NAME: *Liquidambar styraciflua*
HEIGHT: 100-125′
SPREAD: 30-60′
ZONE: 4
FORM: Tall tree, often with a narrow crown

Culture. Grows best in a loose, acid soil but will adapt to most soil conditions except extreme alkalinity (pH greater than 75). Iron chlorosis often occurs under the latter cirsumstances.

Suggested Uses. Shade tree.

Flowers. Insignificant.

Fruit. Round, 1½-inch diameter ball which may become a nuisance in lawns.

Foliage. Deciduous, beautiful yellow to dark purple fall color.

Remarks. Young twigs often have wing-like appendages. This tree is readily available in most nurseries, although seedlings are most commonly offered. Several varieties have been named but more varieties especially adapted to the South should be selected. There are several other species

of Liquidambar, including the Formosa Sweetgum (*L. formosana*) and the Chinese Sweetgum (*L. orientalis*). Of these two species, the former seems to be the best adapted. The Chinese Sweetgum often defoliates in late summer due to fungal leaf spot; it then puts on new leaves which are killed by frost before they have an opportunity to do much more than drain the tree's system of carbohydrates.

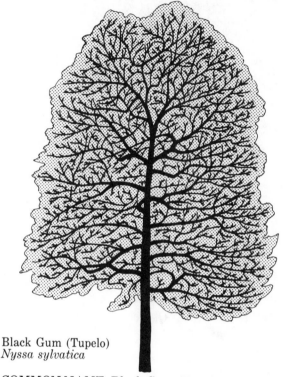

Black Gum (Tupelo)
Nyssa sylvatica

COMMON NAME: Black Gum (Tupelo)
SCIENTIFIC NAME: *Nyssa sylvatica*
HEIGHT: 90′
SPREAD: 30-50′
ZONE: 4
FORM: Rounded crown in the open; upright, columnar under forest conditions

Culture. This tree grows best in sandy, acid soils in high rainfall areas, but it will establish in clay soils that aren't extremely alkaline (pH greater than 7.5). Large specimens may be difficult to transplant but smaller specimens transplant easily.

Suggested Uses. Shade tree for fall color.

Flowers. Insignificant.

Fruit. Bluish-black fruit is produced on female trees and may be rather bad about staining cars, etc., parked underneath them.

Foliage. Deciduous; brilliant red in the fall.

Remarks. The Black Gum is not readily available in most nurseries.

White Oak
Quercus alba

COMMON NAME: White Oak
SCIENTIFIC NAME: *Quercus alba*
HEIGHT: 120′
SPREAD: 50-75′
ZONE: 3
FORM: Large, round-headed shade tree

Culture. Usually found on deep, rich soils; difficult to transplant except when young.

Suggested Uses. Majestic, long-lived shade tree.

Foliage. Deciduous; often colors a reddish-orange in northern regions of the South.

Remarks. This beautiful shade tree should be used more where small sizes can be planted or where existing specimens can be saved from construction damage.

Overcup Oak *(Q. lyrada)*, Swamp Chestnut Oak *(Q. michauxi)* and Post Oak *(Q. stellata)* are other members of the White Oak family which have potential for greater use in the South. The Post Oak is widely found growing in native stands in the South. Although its culture has been limited, some attempt should be made to save existing specimens that are most valuable to the landscape. Post Oaks are very sensitive to construction damage, and they often die three to five years after the home is built. Protection against fill dirt damage to the roots combined with pruning to compensate for a loss of root system will help save these trees (see pages 23-27).

Bald Cypress
Taxodium distichum

COMMON NAME: Bald Cypress
SCIENTIFIC NAME: *Taxodium distichum*
HEIGHT: 130′
SPREAD: 50-75′
ZONE: 4
FORM: Massive tree when older; juvenile growth habit is pyramidal, becoming slender and flat-topped when mature.

Culture. This tree is commonly found in swampy areas, but it will grow under dry land conditions.

Suggested Uses. Large, light shade tree primarily for parks and expansive open areas.

Foliage. Deciduous, fine-textured, pinkish-brown fall color.

Remarks. Bald Cypress is a beautiful tree, and even though it's fast-growing it lives to an old age. Unfortunately, it generally becomes much too large for most home landscapes, but it suffers from relatively few pests. Bagworms are sometimes a problem. There are several other species, including the Montezuma Bald Cypress *(T. mucronatum)*, which tends to be more evergreen, and the Pond Bald Cypress, which is sometimes described as a separate species *(T. ascendens)*, but is similar to the common Bald Cypress. All three of these species produce knee-like projections from the roots, especially when grown in very moist soil conditions.

Green Ash
Fraxinus pennsylvanica

COMMON NAME: Green Ash
SCIENTIFIC NAME: *Fraxinus pennsylvanica*
HEIGHT: 60-100′
SPREAD: 20-40′
ZONE: 2
FORM: Large, rounded-crown shade tree

Culture. Widely adapted to a variety of soil types.

Suggested Uses. Fast-growing shade tree.

Flowers. Most flowers are insignificant; however, one ash variety, *F. cuspidata*, has showy white fragant flowers.

Fruit. Most cultivated species may be either male or female trees, and the females may produce copious amounts of messy seed.

Foliage. Deciduous.

Remarks. A number of Ash species, in addition to the Green Ash, have potential. These include: White Ash *(F. americana)*, Pumpkin Ash *(F. tomentosa*, a wet soil species), Berlandier Ash *(F. berlandieriana)*, Carolina Ash *(F. caroliniana)*, Texas Ash *(F. texensis)* definitely a species worthy of more cultivation, and the Velvet Ash or Arizona Ash *(F. velutina)*. This latter species is one of the most commonly cultivated trees in the Houston,

Texas area. It is easily transplanted but, unfortunately, it is very susceptible to several diseases and tree borers. As a result, it is short-lived, and rather than becoming an asset to the landscape it becomes a liability within about 5 to 10 years.

Sweet Bay Magnolia
Magnolia virginiana

COMMON NAME: Sweet Bay Magnolia
SCIENTIFIC NAME: *Magnolia virginiana*
HEIGHT: 60′
SPREAD: 20-30′
ZONE: 5
FORM: Slender, deciduous-to-evergreen, coarse-textured tree

Culture. Usually growing in wet, sandy, acid soils as an understory species; thus it is tolerant of partial shade.

Suggested Uses. Specimen tree.

Flowers. Flowers are smaller than the Southern Magnolia but are rather fragrant.

Fruit. Bright red seeds are born in cones much like those of the Southern Magnolia, but smaller.

Foliage. The foliage on most species is deciduous, but trees from Alabama may be more evergreen. They are characteristically very prominent when a breeze is blowing through the forest, making the silvery underside of the leaves quite noticeable.

Remarks. Sweet Bay Magnolias are not readily available in nurseries, but they certainly deserve to be, especially in improved forms. The Sweet Bay Magnolia has been crossed with a number of other Magnolia species, and hybrid varieties are available.

Spraying Fruit and Nut Trees

Insects and diseases reduce the quality and quantity of fruits and nuts harvested each year by homeowners. A few carefully timed applications of fungicides and insecticides used in combination with certain cultural practices can reduce insects and diseases.

Cultural Practices

Healthy plants are less susceptible to insect and disease attack. Follow a well-balanced fertility program; select well-adapted varieties and practice proper pruning and other cultural practices conducive to optimum tree growth.

Proper clean-up around trees is extremely important in reducing plum curculio, hickory shuckworm, brown rot of peach, and pecan scab.

Pesticide Safety

Before using any pesticide, carefully read its entire label. Note any special precautions, such as the need to wear special protective clothing when applying the chemical. Take necessary precautions in pesticide applications to avoid any unnecessary chemical contact.

Mix pesticides in a well-ventilated area or out of doors. Avoid chemical contact with skin and do not breathe chemical vapors.

Apply recommended pesticide dosages. Using less pesticide than recommended may result in poor control, and using more than recommended may result in excessive residue or plant damage.

Store pesticides in a secure area away from pets and children. Prepare only the amount of pesticide for an application. Properly dispose of any unused diluted sprays or pesticide containers and never store pesticides in unmarked containers.

Spray Equipment

A number of sprayers on the market satisfactorily apply insecticides and fungicides to plants. Pressure-type sprayers range in size from 1 to 10 gallons. Because of cost and handling ease, most homeowners prefer 2½ to 3-gallon sizes. Hose-on sprayers are least expensive but require a high volume of water, moderate pressure, and a convenient water outlet.

Once a sprayer has been used, it becomes a used pesticide container and requires proper handling and storage. Proper cleaning will prolong its life. Applying insecticides and fungicides with a sprayer previously used to apply herbicides may cause plant damage.

Spray Schedule for Pecans

Pesticide	Dosage	Amount per 3 gal. water	When to apply
Dormant oil	97% oil emulsion	¾ pt.	Apply in January or February for the control of scale and phylloxera.
Pre-pollination	zinc sulfate 68% W.P.*	6 tsp.	Apply about 3 weeks after bud breaks. For control of rosette, pecan scab and foliage feeding insects.
	+		
	Cyprex® 65% W.P.	5 tbsp.	
	or benomyl 50% E.C.	1½ tbsp.	
	+		
	Malathion® 50% E.C.**	8¹⁄₁₀ tbsp.	
	or Guthion® 12% E.C.	4½ tbsp.	
Casebearer spray	Same combination of materials as used for pre-pollination.		Apply in late April or early May for control of pecan nut casebearer, pecan scab, and rosette.
Second generation casebearers	Same combination of materials as used for pre-pollination		Apply 42 days after first casebearer spray. For control of pecan nut casebearer, foliage feeding insects, rosette and pecan scab.
Foliage diseases (scab)	Benomyl 50% W.P.	1½ tbsp.	Apply when pecan kernels enter water stage (mid July-mid August, depending upon location in state).
Hickory shuckworm and foliage diseases (scab)	Benomyl 50% W.P. + Guthion® 12% E.C.	1½ tbsp. 4½ tbsp.	Apply about second week in August. For control of hickory shuckworm and fall foliage diseases.
Foliage feeders	Malathion® 50% E.C.	8 tbsp.	Apply when excessive leaf damage occurs.
Aphids and mites	Guthion® 12% E.C. or	3 tbsp.	Apply when aphids or mites begin to appear on foliage. Malathion® effective on aphids only.

*W.P. = Wettable powder
**E.C. = emulsifiable concentrate

Spray Schedule for Peaches and Plums

Pesticide	Dosage	Amount per 3 gal. water	When to apply
IMPORTANT: Do not apply insecticides within 3 days of harvesting plums or within 7 days of harvesting peaches.			
Dormant oil	97% oil emulsion	½ pt.	Apply in December or January for control of scale.
Pink bud	Captan 50% W.P.	3 tbsp.	For control of plum curculio and brown rot.
	or wettable sulfur	7 tbsp.	
	or benomyl 50% W.P.	1½ tbsp.	
	+		
	Malathion® 50% E.C.	8 tbsp.	
Petal-fall spray	Same as pink bud		For control of plum curculio, brown rot, scab. Apply when 75% of petals have fallen. Benomyl not cleared at this period.
First cover spray	Same as pink bud		Apply 10 to 14 days after petal-fall spray. Benomyl not cleared at this period.
Second cover spray	Same as pink bud		Apply 10 to 14 days after first cover spray. Benomyl not cleared at this period.
Third cover spray	Same as pink bud		May be necessary in some late maturing varieties. Benomyl not cleared at this period.
Pre-harvest	Captan 50% W.P.	3 tbsp.	Apply 1 day prior to first harvest for fruit rots.
	or wettable sulfur	7 tbsp.	
	or benomyl 50% W.P.	1½ tbsp.	

The information given herein is for educational purposes only. Reference to commercial products or trade names is made with the understanding that no discrimination is intended and no endorsement by the Cooperative Extension Service is implied.

Water Oak
Quercus nigra

COMMON NAME: Water Oak
SCIENTIFIC NAME: *Quercus nigra*
HEIGHT: 75'
SPREAD: 40-50'
ZONE: 6
FORM: Round-topped shade tree

Culture. Widely adapted to many soils, including those that are poorly drained, but it is prone to iron chlorosis in alkaline soils.

Suggested Uses. Relatively fast-growing shade tree.

Foliage. Foliage is deciduous but slow to fall.

Remarks. This is one of the most readily available of all oak trees but, as with any species, problems will arise if enough of them are grown. Yellowing due to iron chlorosis and a small gall wasp which attacks the twigs of the tree, seem to be common problems. In addition, a disease called "leaf blister" is also common. The Willow Oak *(Q. phellos)* is similar in its faster growth rate. It has a tendency to have chlorotic foliage and is often a much larger tree, sometimes attaining a height of 130 feet.

Shumard Oak
Quercus shumardii

COMMON NAME: Shumard Oak

SCIENTIFIC NAME: *Quercus shumardii*
HEIGHT: 120'
SPREAD: 50-75'
ZONE: 3
FORM: Large oval shade tree

Culture. Adapted to many soils and growing conditions. More tolerant of alkaline soils and thus less subject to iron chlorosis than the Pin Oak *(Q. palustris)*.

Suggested Uses. Large shade tree.

Foliage. Deciduous, with generally good reddish-brown fall color.

Remarks. This is a much-neglected species of oak, although it is not entirely lacking in the nursery trade. Another similar species, the Nuttall Oak *(Q. nutallii)*, is found in the eastern range of the southern U.S. Because it is often found in poorly drained, tight soils, it is particularly adapted to tight clays of many areas of the Gulf Coast. Nuttall Oak is rare in the nursery trade but should be grown and developed to obtain improved varieties.

SPREAD: 40-50'
ZONE: 6
FORM: Rounded, spreading

Culture. Widely adapted to a variety of soils and growing conditions.

Fruit. A rather large quantity of good-size acorns is produced. They are sweet and make excellent wildlife forage.

Foliage. Shiney, green, deciduous.

Remarks. This species from the Orient deserves more attention for use in the South. At least two other oriental species, *Q. chenii* and *Q. acuta*, do well in the South, but they are quite rare. There are so many oaks with potential for southern landscapes that an entire book could be written on the subject.

Japanese Zelkova
Zelkova serrata

COMMON NAME: Japanese Zelkova
SCIENTIFIC NAME: *Zelkova serrata*
HEIGHT: 50-60'
SPREAD: 25-35'
ZONE: 4
FORM: Vase-shaped, medium-size shade tree

Culture. Widely adapted.

Suggested Uses. This is a nice size tree for today's smaller landscapes.

Sawtooth Oak
Quercus acutissima

COMMON NAME: Sawtooth Oak
SCIENTIFIC NAME: *Quercus acutissima*
HEIGHT: 50'

Foliage. Deciduous, elm-like yellow fall color is sometimes achieved.

Remarks. This species and another, *Z. carpinflora,* are not readily available but can be obtained and could be used more in the fall. The latter species often has red fall color though it is even less well known than *Z. serrata.* These trees are not susceptible to Dutch Elm Disease. Currently, this doesn't mean much since Dutch Elm Disease is not a problem in most of the South.

Cedar Elm
Ulmus crassifolia

COMMON NAME: Cedar Elm
SCIENTIFIC NAME: *Ulmus crassifolia*
HEIGHT: 80′
SPREAD: 30-40′
ZONE: 6
FORM: Deciduous shade tree

Culture. Tolerant of a variety of soil types.

Suggested Uses. Shade tree.

Seed. Produced in the fall.

Foliage. Small, typical, elm-shaped leaves; a yellow to russet brown fall color is typical.

Remarks. This tree is not readily available in nurseries but is sometimes offered as a large transplanted specimen; it is an excellent tree which deserves more attention. Small twigs often have woody, wing-like appendages. The Winged Elm *(U. alata)* has more prominent appendages and produces seed in the spring.

Pecan
Carya illinoensis

COMMON NAME: Pecan
SCIENTIFIC NAME: *Carya illinoensis*
HEIGHT: 125-150′
SPREAD: 50-75′
ZONE: 7
FORM: Broad rounded crown

Culture. Pecan is best adapted to deep river bottom soils but will grow in most areas where the tap root can develop unimpeded by rock or impervious soil layers.

Suggested Uses. Large shade tree

Flowers. Flowering in Pecan trees is of two basic types: *protandrous* varieties, which shed their pollen prior to the time that the female flowers (the small pecans) are receptive and the *protogynous* varieties, which shed their pollen after the female flowers are receptive. If native Pecans are within a mile of a tree to be planted, pollination is usually not a problem; however, when a tree is too isolated, it may be necessary either to plant two complementary trees one protandrous and one protogynous or to graft complementary varieties on one tree. Examples of Pecan varieties which fall into the two categories are:

Protandrous Varieties (pollen first)

Desirable: A large pecan of high kernel quality and good disease resistance. It is a good producer, yielding every year rather than alternate years. Desirable takes approximaetly eight years to come into

(Text continued on page 67)

Pecan Trees

Because they have a long taproot, planting and training pecan trees requires special treatment. Proper planting and training of pecan trees is one of the most important practices in a complete orchard management program. The pecan has gained the reputation of being a difficult tree to transplant yet we have growers who plant thousands of trees with less than a 2 percent loss. The three keys to success in transplanting pecan trees are as follows:

1. Obtain vigorous and fresh pecan nursery stock.
2. Keep root system moist at all times.
3. Reduce the budded or grafted top by a third to a half at time of planting.

The accompanying set of drawings and descriptive captions are designed to outline the basic steps in transplanting and training pecan nursery stock.

1. Obtain good trees. Sturdy, vigorous trees from a reliable nursery source should be used. The root system should be free of crown gall or nematode damage and the top should be well grown and must be identified correctly as to the variety desired. A moderate-sized nursery tree will suffer less "transplant shock" and usually will become established and grow off faster than a large tree.

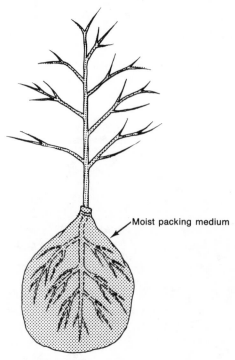

Moist packing medium

2. Keep roots moist. Keep root system moist at all times. Dampen packing media when trees arrive. Plant immediately or place in cold storage. If trees must be held several days, heel them in with moist soil.

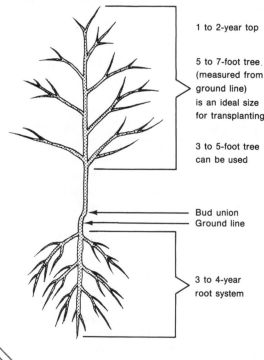

1 to 2-year top

5 to 7-foot tree (measured from ground line) is an ideal size for transplanting

3 to 5-foot tree can be used

Bud union
Ground line

3 to 4-year root system

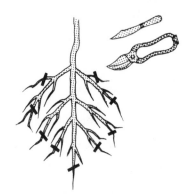

3. Trim root system. Cut off all broken and bruised roots with sharp shears or knife. Most new roots develop on side roots and not more than 10 inches from the tap. Examine the roots closely to assure freedom of serious disease or insect infestation.

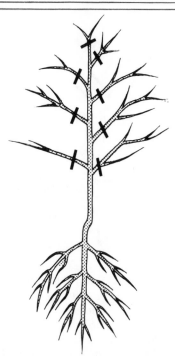

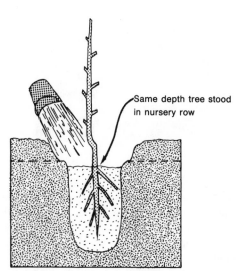

Same depth tree stood
in nursery row

4. Prune top. Remove a third to half of top portion of tree to compensate for the loss of a major part of the functioning root system when tree was dug. If nursery tree has light or no branching, cut off a third to half of the main trunk (whip).

6. Plant tree. Set tree at same depth it stood in nursery row. Arrange roots in their natural position. Fill hole about three-fourths full of friable top soil. Work soil around roots. Pour water into hole to settle soil, eliminate air pockets and keep roots moist.

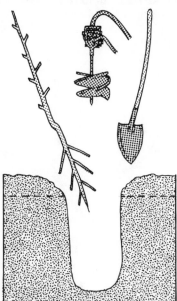

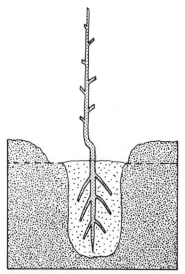

5. Dig hole. The hole should be just wide and deep enough to accommodate the root system of the tree without bending any of the roots. If the soil is so heavy-textured or so devoid of fertility to require digging a large hole, it is not suitable for the growing of pecans on a commercial basis. A power-driven auger, 12 to 18 inches in diameter, is an excellent implement for digging tree planting holes when a sizeable orchard is being set.

7. Finish filling hole. Use loose topsoil to finish filling the hole. Leave soil unpacked on surface to allow easy penetration of water from rain or irrigation. Leave basin to facilitate watering young tree.

(Continued on next page)

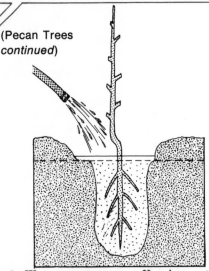

8. Water young tree. Keeping optimum soil moisture levels in the root zone of the young tree is highly essential the first season. The functioning root system is limited at this time. The basin area should be hoed regularly to keep down grass and weeds and to prevent crusting of the soil surface. A heavy mulch may be used for this purpose.

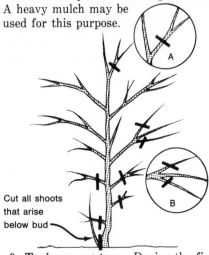

Cut all shoots that arise below bud

9. Train young tree. During the first and second growing seasons, let all shoots from buds on trunk (above union) grow. When shoots on the lower portion of the trunk start vigorous growth, cut them back to a length of 4 to 6 inches and keep them at this length. This "trashy trunk" method of training will protect trunk from sunscald and from wind damage. It will make the trunk increase diameter and strength at a much faster rate. Cut off all water sprouts or suckers that develop below the bud union.

Eliminate "Y" crotches by cutting one of the forks back or completely off. (See inset A.) Correct "crows feet" crotches where three or more limbs arise near the same point, by leaving one growing intact and then cut the others back or off. (See inset B.)

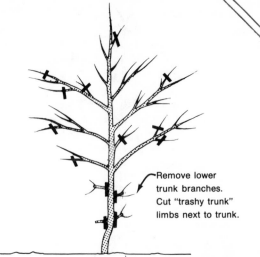

Remove lower trunk branches. Cut "trashy trunk" limbs next to trunk.

10. Prune pecan trees. Continue to eliminate "Y" crotches and "crows feet" as tree grows. This will help build strong wide-angle crotches. The top at the end of the second or third growing seasons can shade the trunk; the trunk then will be strong enough to withstand wind drift so that the branches on the lower part of the trunk may be removed. The desired height of the permanent lower limbs on a pecan tree will be determined by the climate, spacing, and cultural procedures. It usually is not advisable to have permanent scaffold limbs lower than 5 to 6 feet.

This pruning is done during the growing season. Foliage intentionally is not shown for purposes of clarity.

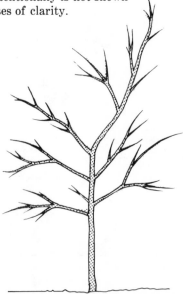

11. Results of proper planting and training. A pecan tree that is trained correctly in the early growing seasons will develop a good system of scaffold limbs. This strong framework of branches can withstand high winds, ice and snow, and the weight of heavy crop loads.

(PECANS *continued from page 63*)

production. Under extremely fast growing conditions it will break with heavy foliage, high rain and wind. Desirable is one of the leading commercial varieties in the Southeast.

Caddo: A medium-size Pecan of high kernel quality and good disease resistance. It is a heavy producer of regular crops. It matures at mid season and the trees come into production in approximately six years.

Cape Fear: A medium-size Pecan of fair kernel quality and good disease resistance. It is productive and comes into production in approximately six years. Cape Fear is being planted in many commercial operations in the Southeast.

Cheyenne: A medium-size Pecan with excellent kernel quality. Although this pecan was originally intended for Central and West Texas planting, it has shown good disease resistance in Galveston County, Texas and is worthy of trial planting in other areas of the South. It is extremely precocious—bearing good crops within four to five years. The blunt, rounded nuts are easy to shell with a 57-61 percent kernel.

Protogynous Varieties (nutlets first)

Choctaw: A large pecan of excellent kernel quality and good disease resistance. It is productive and comes into production in approximately eight years. The nuts mature in the mid season and the tree is vigorous. A small percentage of Choctaw nuts will split on years when a dry summer is followed by an extremely wet autumn.

Mohawk: A large Pecan of good kernel quality and good disease resistance. It is a good producer and the nuts mature early in the season. Mohawk nuts will split on years when a dry summer is followed by an extremely wet autumn.

Mahan: A large Pecan of fair kernel quality and good disease resistance. It is a good producer in the first 15 to 20 years and comes into production in approximately six years. Mahan makes an excellent filler

tree, which should be removed after kernel quality fails.

Chickasaw: A small Pecan of good kernel quality and good disease resistance. It is a heavy producer and comes into production in approximately four years. Chickasaw is a 1972 U.S.D.A. release variety which is showing strong potential for the Gulf Coast, East Texas and the Southeast.

Shawnee: A medium-size Pecan with excellent kernel quality. The somewhat elongate nuts run about 60 percent kernel. This variety has shown excellent disease resistance in Harris County, Texas.

Fruit. Pecan nuts vary considerably among native varieties. Though most people want to plant large pecan trees, it is generally agreed that the small natives seem to have the best flavor and the highest oil content. Perhaps the best solution is to settle for those medium-size Pecans, such as 'Caddo,' 'Shawnee' or 'Sioux,' with a premium quality kernel that have been developed for the shelling industry.

Foliage. Deciduous.

Remarks: Pecans need regular maintenance if they are to produce good crops yearly. Some varieties, such as 'Choctaw' and 'Chickasaw,' respond well to a technique called tip pruning. Using this system, about 6 inches of the growing points all over the tree are cut back each year to force more lateral branching and more potential fruit-producing buds. This also tends to dwarf the tree and make it easier to care for. While this system was originally intended to be used in high-density orchard planting situations, it is also worthwhile for the homeowner. The spray schedule on page 60 is a minimum for production of pecans under home yard situations in the South.

Small to Medium Evergreen Trees

Gulf Coast Juniper *(pictured on next page)*
Juniperus silicicola

COMMON NAME: Ashe Juniper
SCIENTIFIC NAME: *Juniperus silicicola*

HEIGHT: 30′
SPREAD: 15-20′
ZONE: 6
FORM: Typical flame-shaped juniper

Gulf Coast Juniper

Culture. Tolerant of high humidity and widely adapted to southern growing conditions.

Suggested Uses. As a screen or left in natural plantings.

Bark. Peels off in strips.

Foliage. Narrow-leafed evergreen.

Remarks. Nurseries offer many Juniper species, some of which are fairly well-adapted to the lower South, but many, such as cultivars of Rocky Mountain Juniper *(J. scopulorum)* and the Eastern Red Cedar *(J. virginia)*, are often ill-adapted. Junipers are particularly susceptible to spider mite damage during the heat of summer. There are several native species adapted to the South, but they haven't been propagated extensively.

Yaupon
Ilex vomitoria

COMMON NAME: Yaupon

SCIENTIFIC NAME: *Ilex vomitoria*
HEIGHT: 25'
SPREAD: 10-15'
ZONE: 7
FORM: Small single or multi-trunked tree or large shrub.

Culture. Readily adapted to a variety of soil types.

Suggested Uses. As a specimen plant or a screen plant.

Fruit. Male and female trees exist; females produce berries. Male trees are necessary, though, and one or two in a naturalized planting will insure a good fruit set. In addition to the common red fruit varieties, there is also a yellow-fruited Yaupon.

Foliage. Fine-textured evergreen.

Remarks. There are many varieties of Yaupon, including: Weeping Yaupon, Yellowberry Yaupon and Dwarf Yaupon (a shrub).

There are relatively few insect and disease pests, though leaf miners sometimes damage the leaves in early spring. Several applications of diazinon should minimize problems with this pest.

Glossy Privet
Ligustrum lucidum

COMMON NAME: Glossy Privet
SCIENTIFIC NAME: *Ligustrum lucidum*
HEIGHT: 30'
SPREAD: 15-20'
ZONE: 7
FORM: Evergreen tree

Culture. Widely adapted to most soils. Foliar leaf spot due to a fungus is becoming more common.

Suggested Uses. As a large screen plant or as a small evergreen shade tree.

Foliage. Evergreen.

Remarks. This plant is often planted as a hedge, but, because of its vigor, it gets out of bounds and makes a small tree.

Silverdollar Eucalyptus
Eucalyptus cinerea

COMMON NAME: Silverdollar Eucalyptus
SCIENTIFIC NAME: *Eucalyptus cinerea*
HEIGHT: 10-25'
SPREAD: 10-20'
ZONE: 9
FORM: Round-topped evergreen tree

Culture. Adaptable to most soil types, however, because of the dense crown and relatively week trunk, it is necessary to stake or guywire this tree for a number of years before it will hold up on its own. Pruning to thin out some of the branches and reduce the wind load will also help, but because of the vigorous growth that this tree makes, especially along the Gulf Coast area (which is the northern range of its hardiness), it simply grows too well and produces too much foliage for the trunk to support during heavy winds.

Suggested Uses. An accent tree where a source of foliage for indoor arrangements is desired.

Foliage. Evergreen, almost circular and attached to the stem without a petiole.

Remarks. Many Eucalyptus species have been tried along the Gulf Coast. Most either die back completely or are severely damaged every few years during a hard winter. The Bluegum *(E. globulus)* is commonly grown in the Houston,

Texas area, but it is one of those that is severely damaged. Several other species include: Cider Gum *(E. gunni)*, White Ironbark *(E. leucoxylon)* and Snow Gum *(E. niphophila)* are reported to be quite hardy, but the abundant rainfall we often receive in late summer, especially along the Gulf Coast, keeps these trees growing, making them more susceptible to a heavy frost than they might be if a hardening off period of less water and gradually cooler temperatures preconditioned them to this type of weather.

Japanese Yew
Podocarpus macrophylla

COMMON NAME: Japanese Yew
SCIENTIFIC NAME: *Podocarpus macrophylla*
HEIGHT: 50'
SPREAD: 10-15'
ZONE: 8
FORM: Upright, like an exclamation mark

Culture. Appreciates a soil which has been prepared with several inches of organic matter, such as pine bark or peat moss. Very sensitive to wet soil.

Fruit. Green, grape-like fruit on female trees.

Foliage. Fine-textured evergreen.

Remarks. This plant can be used as a shrub, but it is often seen as a large, upright, columnar tree, particularly around older landscapes. It is sometimes attacked by aphids in the spring.

Cherry Laurel
Prunus caroliniana

COMMON NAME: Cherry Laurel
SCIENTIFIC NAME: *Prunus caroliniana*
HEIGHT: 20-40'
SPREAD: 15-25'
ZONE: 7
FORM: Evergreen tree or large shrub.

Culture. Widely adapted to southern soil types.

Suggested Uses. As a large evergreen tree or screen plant.

Flowers. Flowers come very early, in late January or February and, though not strikingly prominent, they are noticeable in small, white racemes.

Remarks. This plant has been worked with to some extent and several named varieties are available, including: 'Bright'N Tight,' 'Otto Luykens' and 'Zabeliana.' The last two are *P. laurocerasus*, (Cherry Laurel) a European species. Another Cherry species adapted to the South is the Black Cherry *(P. serotina)*, with more prominent white flowers in racemes 4 to 6 inches long. This is a long-lived, hardy tree.

Citrus
Citrus sp.

COMMON NAME: Citrus
SCIENTIFIC NAME: Citrus sp.

HEIGHT: 10-25'
SPREAD: 10-20'
ZONE: 8-9
FORM: Rounded evergreen tree

Culture. Adapted to a wide variety of soil types, but most citrus species should be grafted or budded onto Trifoliate Orange root stock, especially if the soil is a tight clay. Plants must be grown in full sun for maximum production.

Suggested Uses. Ornamental fruit tree.

Flowers. White, extremely fragrant; important in many areas as a source of nectar for bees.

Fruit. Variable: oranges, tangerines, lemons, grapefruits and hybrids.

Foliage: Evergreen.

Remarks. The primary pest of citrus is the white fly. There are other potential dangers including several diseases and russet mites which may attack the fruit, but white flies are by far the most serious pest. Control requires applications of a summer oil plus malathion in the spring, midsummer, and again in the fall. Dormant oil applications may be helpful during the winter; however, they should not be applied when temperatures below 40° are expected within 48 hours. There are many varieties of citrus which can be grown along the Gulf Coast, and one, 'Chang Sha,' may be grown as far north as Ft. Worth. Some of the other citrus varieties worthy of consideration are: 'Ichang' Lemon, *Citrus Taiwanica*, 'Fairchild' Tangerine, Satsuma, and Ponkan Honey Orange.

American Holly
Ilex opaca

COMMON NAME: American Holly
SCIENTIFIC NAME: *Ilex opaca*

HEIGHT: 25'
SPREAD: 10-15'
ZONE: 6
FORM: Dense evergreen tree

Culture. Requires a rich acid soil for best growth.

Suggested Uses. Large specimen tree or background screening plant.

Fruit. Only female cultivars produce fruit, but the male is also necessary for good pollination. Many cultivars are available, including: female-'Croonenburg,' 'East Palatlea,' 'Savannah' and 'Hume #2.'

Foliage. Evergreen, spiney.

Remarks. The American Holly is a tradition in the South, and there many hybrid varieties, such as Foster's Holly, *(I. opaca* x *I. cassine)* that also make excellent trees. Another interesting holly species which should be considered because of its tremendous fruitfulness is the Rotunda Holly *(I. rotunda)*. This tree grows about 25 feet tall, with foliage that looks somewhat like that of a Ligustrum.

Large Evergreen Trees

Anaqua
Ehretia anacua

COMMON NAME: Anaqua
SCIENTIFIC NAME: *Ehretia anacua*
HEIGHT: 35-50'
SPREAD: 25-35'
ZONE: 9
FORM: Semi-evergreen, round-top tree.

Culture. Although this tree grows in a variety of places, including dry poor soils as well as rich river valleys, it attains its largest size where good soil and adequate rainfall are available.

Suggested Uses. Small to medium-size semi-evergreen tree.

Flowers. Fragrant; white panicles 2 to 3 inches long.

Fruit. ¼ to ⅓ inch in diameter, round and yellowish-orange, rather ornamental.

Remarks. This tree should be used more than it is since it has relatively few pests and makes a handsome specimen. In addition, the fruit is valuable forage for wildlife.

Japanese Black Pine
Pinus thunbergii

COMMON NAME: Japanese Black Pine
SCIENTIFIC NAME: *Pinus thunbergii*
HEIGHT: 30'
SPREAD: 15'
ZONE: 5
FORM: Irregular, narrow-leafed evergreen tree

Culture. Adapted to a wide variety of soils and tolerant of salt.

Suggested Uses. Small accent specimen, particularly useful where an Oriental landscaping theme is desired.

Foliage. Needles 3 to 5 inches long, two needles in a bundle.

Remarks. This tree is adapted to a wide area of the U.S., and although it does grow in the lower South (along the Gulf Coast), it doesn't make the outstanding specimen it will in other parts of the South. It is extremely easy to train to bonsai form. Another introduced species is the Italina Stone Pine *(P. pinea)*, an interesting small pine that produces a large edible seed. It, too, has a picturesque growth habit, having rather umbrella-like branches.

Spruce Pine
Pinus glabra

COMMON NAME: Spruce Pine
SCIENTIFIC NAME: *Pinus glabra*
HEIGHT: 50-80′
SPREAD: 20-30′
ZONE: 7
FORM: Narrow-leaved, pyramidal evergreen

Culture. Best adapted to sandy soils but will establish in fairly tight soils that aren't extremely alakaline (pH greater than 7.5).

Suggested Uses. Specimen evergreen tree or large screen plant. Since it has short needles and a pyramidal form similar to Scotch Pine, when small it can be used as a Christmas tree.

Foliage. Needles 3 inches long in bundles of two.

Remarks. The Spruce Pine is not readily available in the nursery trade, but it should be. There are a number of other native short-needled pines which could be used more in the South, including: Pinyon Pine *(P. edulis)*—a slow-growing pine, with blue-

green needles and large edible nuts that eventually reaches a height of approximately 20 feet; Sand Pine *(P. clausa)*—another short-needled pine, 15 to 20 feet tall; Virginia Pine *(P. virginiana)*—this pine has great potential for use in southern Christmas tree plantations, ultimate height is 30 to 40 feet; and Pond Pine *(P. serotina)*—this pine is adapted to moist, swampy conditions and eventually reaches a height of about 40 feet.

Loblolly Pine
Pinus taeda

COMMON NAME: Loblolly Pine
SCIENTIFIC NAME: *Pinus taeda*
HEIGHT: 100′
SPREAD: 25-35′
ZONE: 6
FORM: Large, oval, narrow-leaved evergreen

Culture. Best adapted to sandy acid soils.

Suggested Uses. Large evergreen tree.

Foliage. Long needles, usually in clusters of three.

Remarks. The Loblolly Pine is rather susceptible to Pine Tip Moth, and for this reason, Slash Pine, which is similar, has been planted because it is resistant to the moth. Unfortunately, Slash Pine is susceptible to fusiform rust, which is an almost as much of a problem. If Slash Pine is to be used as a substitute for Loblolly Pine, it's important that strains resistant to the fusiform rust be grown. Long-leafed pine, *Pinus palustris*, is another commonly grown long-needle pine, but it is very intolerant of clay soils. Ponderosa Pine *(P. ponderosa)* and Austrian Pine *(P. nigra)* are other long-needle species which can be grown in some areas of the South but which are not adapted to the Gulf Coast area.

Camphor Tree
Cinnamomum camphora

COMMON NAME: Camphor Tree
SCIENTIFIC NAME: *Cinnamomum camphora*
HEIGHT: 40′
SPREAD: 20-30′
ZONE: 9
FORM: Round-topped evergreen tree

Culture. Tolerant of most soil types, though it is subject to iron chlorosis in alkaline pH.

Suggested Uses. Large specimen evergreen tree or large screen plant.

Fruit. Small, round black berry produced in quantities large enough to become a nuisance.

Foliage. Glossy, very aromatic, with a characteristic odor of camphor.

Remarks. This tree makes a beautiful shade tree but may be considered messy because of the large quantities of fruit; it also has a rather shallow root system.

Live Oak
Quercus virginiana

COMMON NAME: Live Oak
SCIENTIFIC NAME: *Quercus virginiana*
HEIGHT: 60′

SPREAD: 50-60′
ZONE: 7
FORM: Wide-spreading with large horizontal branches

Culture. Widely adapted to many areas of the South, but only developing to majestic proportions in the rich soils and humid climate of river valleys and the fertile southeast.

Suggested Uses. Large shade tree.

Foliage. Deciduous, evergreen but becoming sparse in late winter.

Remarks. No doubt there are many superior Live Oak specimens which could be propagated if an efficient means of vegetative propagation were found. Preliminary results at Texas A&M University indicate that Live Oaks can be rooted from vigorous juvenile growth. At least one seedling variety, the Heritage Live Oak, has been promoted as fast-growing, but its real worth is somewhat doubtful.

Deodar Cedar
Cedrus deodara

COMMON NAME: Deodar Cedar
SCIENTIFIC NAME: *Cedrus deodara*
HEIGHT: 40-80′
SPREAD: 20-40′
ZONE: 7
FORM: Narrow-leafed evergreen, pyramidal growth habit, pendulous branches

Culture. Widely adapted to a variety of soil types.

Suggested Uses. Medium to large evergreen.

Foliage. Light grayish-green.

Remarks. The Deodar Cedar does well in the Gulf Coast area, but in more humid regions the top often dies out at 30 to 40 feet, leaving a flat-topped pyramid.

Southern Magnolia
Magnolia grandiflora

COMMON NAME: Southern Magnolia

SCIENTIFIC NAME: *Magnolia grandiflora*
HEIGHT: 90′
SPREAD: 40-60′
ZONE: 7
FORM: Pyramidal evergreen tree

Culture. Fairly tolerant of soil types, but prefers a loose, rich, acid soil with abundant organic matter.

Suggested Uses. Large specimen, flowering evergreen tree.

Flowers. Large, (8 inches in diameter), white and fragrant.

Fruit. Cucumber-like pods which open to reveal red seeds.

Foliage. Coarse, very glossy evergreen.

Remarks. Several varieties are available. Two worth trying are 'St. Mary' and 'Samuel Sommer.' Magnolia has relatively few pests but is sometimes damaged by algal leaf spot, which causes yellowing of the leaves. This is readily controlled with a copper fungicide. Also, it seems that magnolias are especially susceptible to girdling roots. This problem is exacerbated by the common culture of Southern Magnolias in cans. When a girdling root is found, it must be removed to keep it from strangling part of the root system (see page 22).

Palms

PLANTING PALMS

Palms must be planted when the soil is warm. Fibrous palm roots grow from a root collar. When severed, these roots die back completely rather than branch out as most tree roots do. Initiation of new fibrous roots is most rapid when the soil temperature is warm; thus it is a good idea to plant palm trees before September 1 in all but the most tropical areas of the South.

Container-grown palm trees can be more successfully transplanted in cold weather. To prevent damage to tender developing roots, it's important to brace large palms against the wind for one to two years after planting.

Palm trees benefit from a loose soil that has been improved with a generous amount of organic matter. Mixing 1 to 2 inches of pine bark, peat moss or compost into the soil prior to planting is advisable. In areas where soils are tight and rainfall is heavy, setting the tree 1 to 2 inches high is also advisable. In the fall, prior to a hard frost, it's a good idea to mulch the base of the tree in a 2- to 3-foot radius with pine bark or a similar mulch to prevent freeze damage to tender root systems. This, of course, is only necessary with palm species that are marginally hardy in colder regions of the South.

Pindo Palm
Butia capitata

COMMON NAME: Pindo Palm
SCIENTIFIC NAME: *Butia capitata*
HEIGHT: 20′
SPREAD: 10′
ZONE: 9
FORM: Feather-leafed palm

Culture. Tolerant of varying soils.

Suggested Uses. Small to medium-size specimen palm. Except for the fruit, this is not a messy palm.

Flowers. Small, but abundant in large 3-foot long spadices.

Fruit. Orange, date-like with a tart tropical taste. Makes excellent jelly.

Foliage. Feather-shaped leaf, grayish-green.

Remarks. Rather slow-growing, but long-lived and relatively pest-free.

Texas Palmetto
Sabal texana

COMMON NAME: Texas Palmetto
SCIENTIFIC NAME: *Sabal texana*
HEIGHT: 20-40′
SPREAD: 5′

ZONE: 9
FORM: Fan-leafed palm

Culture. Widely adapted to many soil types.

Suggested Uses. Medium-size, accent tree.

Foliage. Huge 4- to 7-foot wide fan-shaped leaves.

Remarks. This tree is one of the best adapted of all to the Gulf Coast, and many of the larger specimens have already been used in landscapes. Because it is rather slow-growing, this palm may begin to disappear from landscapes in favor of faster-growing palms such as the Washingtonias.

Washingtonia Palm
Washingtonia filifera

COMMON NAME: Washingtonia Palm
SCIENTIFIC NAME: *Washingtonia filifera*
HEIGHT: 40′
SPREAD 5-10′
ZONE: 9
FORM: Fan-leafed palm

Culture. Widely adapted to many soil types.

Suggested Uses. As a street planting or border tree.

Foliage. Large, fan-shaped leaves.

Remarks. The *W. filifera* is the hardier of the Washingtonia species, and although it is not as tall and graceful as the *W. robusta*, it should be planted except in areas where temperatures sometimes fall below 25°. *W. filifera* has a thicker, heavier trunk than *W. robusta*.

Chinese Fountain Palm
Livingstona chinensis

COMMON NAME: Chinese Fountain Palm
SCIENTIFIC NAME: *Livingstona chinensis*
HEIGHT: 25′
SPREAD: 5-10′
ZONE: 9
FORM: Fan-leafed palm

Culture. Widely adapted to many soil types.

Suggested Uses. Nice accent plant near the patio.

Foliage. Large, glossy fan-shaped foliage.

Remarks. Somewhat tender in the Houston area; it is best planted in a protected location such as an interior courtyard.

European Fan Palm
Chamaerops humilis

COMMON NAME: European Fan Palm
SCIENTIFIC NAME: *Chamaerops humilis*
HEIGHT: 15′
SPREAD: 10-15′
ZONE: 9
FORM: Large, clump-forming palm

Culture. Widely adapted to many soil types.

Suggested Uses. As a small specimen or screen plant.

Foliage. Fan-shaped leaves.

Remarks. This is one of the hardiest palms and yet it is not offered in nurseries nearly as much as it should be.

Windmill Palm
Trachycarpus fortunei

COMMON NAME: Windmill Palm
SCIENTIFIC NAME: *Trachycarpus fortunei*
HEIGHT: 20′
SPREAD: 5-10′
ZONE: 9
FORM: Slender-trunked, fan-leafed palm

Culture. Widely adapted to many soil types and tolerant of shade.

Suggested Uses. Slow-growing palm for use as a small specimen.

Foliage. Fan-shaped leaves.

Remarks. The trunk of this tree seems to get narrower at the base, sometimes causing growers to wonder if it isn't a bit out of proportion.

Lady Palm
Rhapis excelsa

COMMON NAME: Lady Palm
SCIENTIFIC NAME: *Rhapis excelsa*
HEIGHT: 10′
SPREAD: 10′
ZONE: 9
FORM: Clump-forming

Culture. Does best in shade in a moist fertile soil.

Suggested Uses. Specimen plant in shaded places or in the home.

Foliage. Digitate (finger-like).

Remarks. Seeds are rarely produced, so this tree is often rather expensive because it's generally propagated by division.

Canary Island Date Palm
Phoenix canariensis

COMMON NAME: Canary Island Date Palm
SCIENTIFIC NAME: *Phoenix canariensis*
HEIGHT: 60′

SPREAD: 15-25′
ZONE: 9
FORM: Heavy-trunked, feather-leaved palm

Culture. Tolerant of salt, adapted to many soils, but good drainage is important.

Suggested Uses. This tree is too large for most home landscapes, but it may be used in commercial or public landscaping.

Foliage. Large, feather-shaped leaves.

Remarks. This tree is often planted in smaller home landscapes where it soon becomes much too large, and, unfortunately, it is rather difficult to remove. Though it will grow, the commerical date palm is not an especially attractive palm in humid areas of the South, and it rarely sets fruit.

Other Landscape Trees

No book about trees, even a regional one, can possibly include every species that can be grown in that region. There are a great many species that are as yet untried and unpublicized but which can be used in the South; there are also many species which have minimal value even though they may be widely planted. Some species are better adapted to the North or to northern areas of the South and they may be widely planted in or even native to these areas yet they aren't adapted to the deep South. The following are some of these "other" trees which have received little or no mention in the previous section of this book.

Mimosa or Silk Tree
(Albizia julibrissin)

The Mimosa is a widely planted tree and one that is very attractive when in bloom. It is flat-topped, has an umbrella-crown and very fine-textured foliage. It is a very popular tree because the pink to red pin cushion-like flowers are produced in spring. Unfortunately, this tree is rather short-lived, the blossoms are messy, and it is rather susceptible to Mimosa Wilt and Mimosa Webworm. One variety, 'Charlotte,' is reported to be resistant to Mimosa Wilt but probably won't sur-

vive in an area where an infected tree had to be removed.

Monkey-Puzzle Tree
(Araucaria Araucana)

The Monkey-Puzzle Tree is related to the Norfolk Island Pine but is hardy to at least Zone 7. It is evergreen, with pointed scale-like leaves and weird twisted branches. It is an unsightly though unusual tree.

Arborvitae
Thuja Orientalis

Arborvitae is a commonly planted tree in home landscapes. When young it has an attractive flame shape and bright yellowish-green color. With age, however, it simply becomes a large oval mass of green foliage that is very susceptible to bagworms and spider mite infestations.

Madrone
(Arbutus Texana)

Texas Madrone is a besutiful tree, sometimes called Naked Indian because of the smooth pink bark. Unfortunately, it has been rather difficult to cultivate outside its native range of central and west Texas. Perhaps it requires a special mycorrhizal fungus common to its native soil in order to grow properly. Whatever the difficulty, it is unfortunate that it can't be used more.

Paper Mulberry
(Broussonetia Papyrifera)

The Paper Mulberry is a rather coarse tree that is best adapted to areas where more attractive trees can't be grown. It is sometimes used for quick shade in areas west of Houston, Texas.

Chinese Chestnut
(Castanea mollissima)

The Chinese Chestnut is resistant to chestnut blight and has potential use for in the South. At one time, some work was done with the Chinese Chestnuts for southern use at Auburn University. There may be some remnants of these adapted varieties lingering there.

Carob
(Ceratonia Siliqua)

Often grown as a large shrub, it can be trained to a tree with the lower branches removed. It eventually develops a dense rounded head. Although hardy to 18°, the Carob is not well adapted to areas with frequent rainfall.

Coral Tree
(Erythrina Crista-galli)

The Coral Tree is not hardy much north of Houston, Texas, but it can be grown there, though often frozen back. Spectacular red waxy flowers which look something like a fireman's cap are this tree's main attraction.

American Beech
(Fagus grandiflora)

American Beech is well adapted to many areas of the southeast; it requires a deep, sandy, acid soil and it is a rather large majestic tree not suited to small landscapes.

Chinquapin
(Castanea alnifolia, C. ashei, C. pumila)

These small- to medium-sized, spreading, deciduous trees are well adapted to sandy, acid soils.

The Chinquapins are often multi-trunked, and they produce sweet, edible nuts in the fall. The Florida Chinquapin *(C. alnifolia* var. *floridana)* is particularly suited to landscape use in the South.

Arizona Ash
(Fraxinus velutina)

The Arizona Ash is one of the most commonly planted trees in the South. It grows rather quickly, makes almost instant shade, but after five years it becomes more of a liability than an asset in the landscape. It is very susceptible to borers, has several serious disease problems, and is short-lived. A curious yellow-brown mushroom often comes up all over the lawn where this tree has been planted. It is a mycorrhizal fungus associated only with Ash trees. This fungus cannot be controlled chemically. Removal of the tree is the only way to get rid of it.

Maidenhair Tree
(Ginkgo biloba)

The Maidenhair Tree is fascinating because for many years it was only known through fossils before it was actually discovered in a remote valley in China. It is not well adapted to the lower South; it seems to suffer from the long wet summers, but it can be grown and it is worth planting, especially in Arboretums or on school grounds because of its interesting history.

Honey Locust
(Gleditsia triacanthos)

The Honey Locust, especially the great many thornless varieties, is widely used in the upper South but is not particularly adapted to the lower half of Zone 8 and below.

Dawn Redwood
(Metasequoia glyptostroboides)

The Dawn Redwood, like the Maidenhair, was known in fossils before its discovery in the 1940's in a remote valley in China. It grows very rapidly and is adapted to the South, especially in woodland situations where it has an acid soil and receives some protection from full sun all day.

American Linden
(Tilia americana)

The American Linden is grown to some extent in the South and, in fact, is native as far west in Texas as the Frio River area near Camp Wood in

Lakey, Texas. However, it is not common in this area and it is not readily available in nurseries though it may be worthy of more planting.

Sweet Leaf
(Symplocos tinctoria)

The Sweet Leaf is adapted to deep, rich sandy soils and is commonly found in the southeast. It may be partially evergreen, it makes a large shrub or small tree, and is rather open and spreading. It has limited use as a landscape specimen, but its leaves are interesting because they have a sugary taste. It is relatively unavailable in southern nurseries but should be preserved if it is found growing naturally.

Kentucky Coffee Tree
(Gymnocladus dioica)

The Kentucky Coffee Tree is an interesting long-lived tree, native to rich bottom lands. There are both male and female trees, and in most instances the males are preferred because of the large seed pods and seed produced on female trees. They are not easy to transplant but are worthy of more attention.

Sycamore
(Platanus occidentalis)

The Sycamore grows over a wide range of the U.S., and though it's adapted to the South, it has many serious problems, such as anthracnose, lace bugs, mites, leaf beetles, and the disease sometimes known as live oak decline or persimmon wilt, to which it is extremely susceptible. One variety found growing in Mexico has very large leaves which are predominately white on the underside. It is worth trying in the southwest.

Wright Acacia
(Acacia wrightii)

Wright Acacia is an interesting small, flowering tree for use in areas with limited space. Though it ultimately grows to full size, it is rather slow-growing. The tree is semi-evergreen in the lower South. Wright Acacias are relatively unavailable in the nursery trade but are easily grown from seed. Small plants may be collected, too. Liberal pruning of lower branches, which tend to droop, may be required. Acacia trees are best adapted to areas of good drainage with full sun.

Trinidad Flame Tree
[Calliandra guildingi (tweedii)]

This is a rather open, spreading tree that responds well to informal training against a wall. It is rather hardy from Houston south and probably can be grown further north in protected locations. Brilliant, powder puff-looking red blooms are produced throughout the growing season, and fine-textured Mimosa-like foliage makes the Trinidad Flame Tree especially useful where low maintenance and cleanliness are required.

Texas Ebony
(Pithecellobium flexicaule)

This small, rounded, long-lived tree appreciates well drained soil and a protected location in the northern limits of its hardiness (approximately Houston). The Texas Ebony makes a very attractive small specimen tree. Cream-colored Acacia-like flowers are produced in the early spring; however, in its northern limits the flower buds will often freeze. It has prominent small sharp, spines that are produced along angular branches.

Orchid Trees
(Bauhinia congesta, B. purpurea, B. mexicana, B. forficata)

These small, flowering trees like full sun and a well drained soil. They make excellent specimen trees and produce showy white or purple flowers. Most species have unusual leaves shaped like a cloven hoof.

Tri-foliate Orange
(Poncirus trifoliata)

This small, flowering, thorny tree is very tolerant of varying soil types and does best in full sun. Tri-foliate Orange is usually thought of as a root stock for commercial citrus, but it makes a good ornamental small tree or an impenetrable hedge due to its large thorns. It is deciduous, and its fragrant white flowers are followed by small, edible fruit.

Evergreen Pear
(Pyrus kawakami)

This small, flowering tree is one of the earliest-blooming of all flowering trees. It usually begins blooming in late January or early February in the

Houston area. Although called "Evergreen Pear," the tree is actually deciduous except in tropical areas. It is readily available in many southern nurseries.

Carolina Buckthorn
(Rhamnus caroliniana)

Carolina Buckthorn can be used either as a shrub or as a small tree. It is tolerant of wet soils and it makes an excellent background plant. This is one of the earliest of all fruiting plants to show color. Berries begin to turn red as early as August. Foliage is deciduous, turning yellow in the fall.

Southern Waxmyrtle
(Myrica cerifera)

The Southern Waxmyrtle is a small, multi-stemmed evergreen tree and will grow almost anywhere, being tolerant of tight, wet soils as well as dry soils. Its foliage is very aromatic, and the tree is very serviceable and easy to grow.

Apple
(Malus pumila)

Apple is a medium to large, rounded, flowering and fruiting tree. It has relatively easy culture, though spraying will usually be necessary to protect the fruit from insect and disease damage. We can now produce apples, even in the lower South, with varieties like: 'Anna,' 'Ein Sheimer,' 'Molly's Delicious,' 'Tropical Beauty,' 'Borgden,' 'Wiregrass,' and 'Valmore'.

Devil's Walkingstick
(Aralia spinosa)

This slender, prickly tree is usually found growing in moist soils. Devil's Walkingstick is heavily armed with orange prickles and has uniquely large compound leaves.

Black Walnut
(Junglans nigra)

The Black Walnut is a large, rounded-crown shade tree that is best adapted to deep, fertile, alluvial soils along river bottoms, though it is tolerant of other soil types. The roots of the Black Walnut tree are known to give off a substance which is toxic to some other plants and prevents them from growing around it. The foliage is deciduous, and it is bothered by the same insects and diseases that trouble Pecans; thus it is not always attractive in a landscape.

Several species of Black Walnut can be used for home landscapes, namely, the Texas Black Walnut (J. microcarpa) and the Arizona Black Walnut (J. major), both of which are much smaller trees than J. nigra.

Hickory
(Carya ovata)

This large shade tree requires about the same growing conditions and is susceptible to the same diseases as Pecan. None of the Hickories are readily available in nurseries because of their slow growth and the difficulty of transplanting large specimens; however, it must be remembered that most slow-growing trees are also long-lasting.

Other worthy Hickory species include the Black Hickory (C. texans), the Nutmeg Hickory (C. myristicaformis), and the Pignut Hickory (C. glabra).

Although Pecans can be grafted onto Hickories with occasional success, the nut production from this union is so low that the time and effort are really not justified.

Lime Prickly-Ash
(Zanthoxylum fagara)

Lime Prickly-Ash makes an excellent small evergreen specimen tree. Its fine-textured evergreen leaves, as well as its bark, are used medicinally as a sudorific (perspiration agent) and nerve tonic.

Loquat
(Eriobotrya japonica)

The Loquat is an easily grown coarse-textured evergreen tree. It makes a good small ornamental tree, and produces very fragrant, though inconspicuous, flowers. Rather extreme susceptibility to a prevalent bacterial disease, limits the usefulness of this tree in southern landscapes.

Texas Pistache
(Pistacia texana)

Though Texas Pistache is a small deciduous tree, its leaves are persistent and somewhat evergreen in its southern range (Houston and south). It is easily grown and is particularly well adapted to alkaline soils.

This species is becoming quite rare in Texas, but through the activities of such organizations as the Texas Rare Plant Studies Center, there is now some interest in developing it for southern landscape use.

Florida Anisetree
(Illicium floridanum)

The Florida Annisetree is found in Louisiana east to Florida in moist, swampy areas and has some potential for use as a landscape specimen. This small tree gives the landscape a natural, woodsy effect. It is best adapted to sandy, acid soils. The dark red, star-like flowers are prominent at close range but are barely discernible from a distance.

Bronze Loquat
[Photinia (eribotrya) deflexa (bronze)]

The Bronze Loquat is a small evergreen tree that is easily grown and widely adapted to various soils. It does well in containers. It produces terminal clusters of fragrant white flowers in the spring. The foliage has a showy reddish-bronze color; mature leaves are dark green.

Olive
(Olea europaea)

The Olive is best adapted to dry, sandy soils and full sun. Its form is dense and rounded, except when growing in good soil, when it assumes a more irregular growth habit. This is a good tree for dry, hot areas like the small islands in parking lots. Fruit production is unlikely in the Southeast, however, because of frequent rains and high humidity.

Index